A WOMAN IN THE HOUSE (AND SENATE)

HOW WOMEN CAME TO THE UNITED STATES CONGRESS, BROKE DOWN BARRIERS, AND CHANGED THE COUNTRY

BY ILENE COOPER
ILLUSTRATIONS BY ELIZABETH BADDELEY
FOREWORD BY FORMER U.S. SENATOR OLYMPIA SNOWE

ABRAMS BOOKS FOR YOUNG READERS
NEW YORK

The illustrations in this book were made with pen, ink, and watercolor.

Library of Congress Cataloging-in-Publication Data

Cooper, Ilene.
A woman in the House (and Senate) : how women came to the United States
Congress, broke down barriers, and changed the country / by Ilene Cooper ;
with illustrations by Elizabeth Baddeley.
pages cm
Includes bibliographical references and index.
ISBN 978-1-4197-1036-0 (alk. paper)
1. Women—Political activity—United States—History—Juvenile literature.
2. Women legislators—United States—History—Juvenile literature.
3. United States. Congress—History—Juvenile literature. I. Title.
HQ1236.5.U6C667 2014
320.082—dc23
2013022201

Book design by Sara Corbett

Printed and bound in China
10 9 8 7 6 5 4 3 2 1

Abrams Books for Young Readers are available at special discounts when
purchased in quantity for premiums and promotions as well as fundraising or
educational use. Special editions can also be created to specification. For details,
contact specialsales@abramsbooks.com or the address below.

ABRAMS
THE ART OF BOOKS SINCE 1949

115 West 18th Street
New York, NY 10011
www.abramsbooks.com

FOR MARIYA TIKHONOVA

AND ALL THE YOUNG WOMEN WHO WILL BEND
THE ARC OF HISTORY TOWARD JUSTICE

—I. C.

FOR ZACK

—E. B.

CONTENTS

FOREWORD VI

INTRODUCTION VIII

* * * * * * *

PART 1

"Men, Their Rights and Nothing More; Women, Their Rights and Nothing Less" x

CHAPTER 1 Number One 5

CHAPTER 2 Next Up 10

PART 2

Flash and Crash, 1920–1930 12

CHAPTER 3 Widows (Mostly) 16

CHAPTER 4 . . . and Daughters 23

PART 3

Hard Times: Depression, War, and the Red Menace, 1931–1953 28

CHAPTER 5 The Women of Arkansas 33

CHAPTER 6 Stars! 36

PART 4

Settling Down and Stirring Things Up, 1954–1963 44

CHAPTER 7 Carrying the Banner 49

CHAPTER 8 Missouri and Michigan 53

PART 5

"A Change Is Gonna Come," 1964–1979 56

CHAPTER 9 A Different Kind of Pioneer 61

CHAPTER 10 "Unbought and Unbossed" **63**

CHAPTER 11 Joining Shirley **65**

CHAPTER 12 Two Good Friends **69**

CHAPTER 13 A Woman of Her Time **72**

CHAPTER 14 A Possible Vice President **75**

CHAPTER 15 Pacific State Senator, Prairie State Senator **77**

PART 6

THE CALM BEFORE
THE STORM, 1980–1999 .... **80**

CHAPTER 16 The Year of the Woman **85**

CHAPTER 17 Maine—Two Woman Senators **89**

PART 7

AN UNSETTLING
DECADE, 2000–2010 .... **92**

CHAPTER 18 From One End of Pennsylvania Avenue to the Other . . **97**

CHAPTER 19 The Changing Senate **100**

CHAPTER 20 Madame Speaker **102**

PART 8

WHAT GOES UP MUST COME
DOWN—AND GOES BACK UP! **104**

* * * * * * *

APPENDIX **112**

COMPLETE LIST OF WOMEN IN CONGRESS **119**

ENDNOTES **122**

BIBLIOGRAPHY **126**

PHOTOGRAPHY CREDITS **127**

INDEX **129**

For too long, women in America had to endure the myth of what—or where—a "woman's place" should be. Today, much has changed, and a woman's place is virtually anywhere—including the United States Congress!

A Woman in the House (and Senate) tells the fascinating and important story of this ongoing transformation, taking the reader on a journey from before women's suffrage to a record number of female representatives and senators. With vibrant verbal portraits of trailblazing women, Ilene Cooper brings to life the indispensable significance of women's contributions to Congress and our nation. This book will also inspire and empower America's newest generation to continue the unfinished work of ensuring that more women serve at *all* levels of elective office.

If it is true that we can see farther by standing on the shoulders of giants— and I believe it is—then the role models you will read about here offer many distinguished shoulders on which to climb!

Growing up, I was incredibly fortunate to have the example of Maine's legendary Senator Margaret Chase Smith, who is profiled in these pages. Her life demonstrated that success in public service, or in any endeavor, shouldn't be based on gender but rather on dedication and energy, competence and ability, and sheer determination.

Yet, regrettably, for years women had been the great "silent majority." They were the majority of voters, but their calls for changes in laws and practices discriminatory against women were too often met with silence. It wasn't until women were elected to Congress that their issues finally found a voice.

In 1978, my first year in the House of Representatives, there were only sixteen women out of 435 members of the House, and only one female senator. So we all felt a tremendous obligation to "go to bat" for the women of America. Like many who came before us, as described in this book, there was

OLYMPIA SNOWE

a deep understanding that if we didn't fight for women's issues, no one would.

Incredibly, that was a time in America when child-support enforcement was viewed as strictly a woman's problem. A time when pensions were canceled without a spouse's approval. A time when family and medical leave wasn't the law of the land. A time when women unbelievably were systematically excluded from potentially life-saving clinical medical trials.

But the women of the House and Senate worked together, both Republican and Democrat, to right these wrongs and remove the inequities—proving again that there is no substitute for having women in the arena to drive the agenda!

As you will glean from the profiles encompassed in this book, women also frequently bring a different perspective to decision-making. They tend to be practical, results-oriented, and focused on getting to the bottom line of a problem!

That's one of the reasons it is critical that more women are elected, especially given that today's extreme political partisanship is preventing us from meeting the monumental challenges facing our nation. Another is that, in our representative form of government, shouldn't our governing institutions be more reflective of society as a whole?

The total number of woman senators and representatives in America's history is 296. That's out of a total of 12,099 individuals who have served in Congress. Those women could all sit in the chamber of the House of Representatives . . . with 139 seats to spare! While 101 women serve in Congress in 2013, indisputably there is still significant progress to be made. The stories told here should spark all of us—and particularly girls and women—to close that gender gap.

Ultimately, if we are to celebrate and strengthen the vast array of options available to girls and women today, we must learn about those who fought to give life and reality to our dreams. If we are to attain our fullest potential as a nation and exercise our rights as Americans, we must understand that those rights came to us not by entitlement but by tenacity and perseverance. As *A Woman in the House (and Senate)* conveys with a sense of wit and wonder, we are now the bearers of the torch that so many lit before us, and of their extraordinary legacy, which will forever endure.

OLYMPIA SNOWE

FORMER U.S. SENATOR

UNITED STATES · CAPITOL

THE SENATE SIDE

THE HOUSE SIDE

See that building? The one with the wedding-cake dome? (It's really made of cast iron.) That's the United States Capitol Building. It's the home of the United States Congress.

The United States is governed by three equal branches of government.

* **THE EXECUTIVE BRANCH** Hail to the chief!

* **THE JUDICIAL BRANCH** Nine—count 'em, nine—Supreme Court Judges.

* **THE LEGISLATIVE BRANCH** That's the Congress.

Our Congress has two parts, known as chambers: the Senate and the House of Representatives—"the House," for short.

EXECUTIVE

JUDICIAL

LEGISLATIVE

3 BRANCHES OF GOVERNMENT

The Senate currently has 100 members: two senators from every state in the Union, no matter how big or how small. Each senator is elected for a six-year term.

The House has 435 members. The number of representatives from each state depends on population. The states with the most people have the most representatives. Representatives are elected for a two-year term.

The word "Congress" has another meaning. It's also the name for the two-year period when senators and representatives meet in Washington, D.C., to do their work. Since the founding of our country there have been more than a hundred Congresses.

Guess how many women served in the U.S. Senate and the House of Representatives from the first Congress in 1789 until the 65th Congress began in 1917.

200? 100? 50?

Zero. Nada. None. That's right, there was not one woman senator or member of the House during the first 128 years of our country's history.

What's up with that?

* * * * * *

Each state also has its own version of Congress. Forty-nine of the fifty states have two-chamber legislatures, usually called the Senate and the House of Representatives, though some have other names. Nebraska's legislature has just one body, and it's called the Senate. Although the United States House and Senate did not have a woman representative until 1917, three women were elected to Colorado's House of Representatives in 1894! Colorado was the first state to have woman legislators. But that's another story.

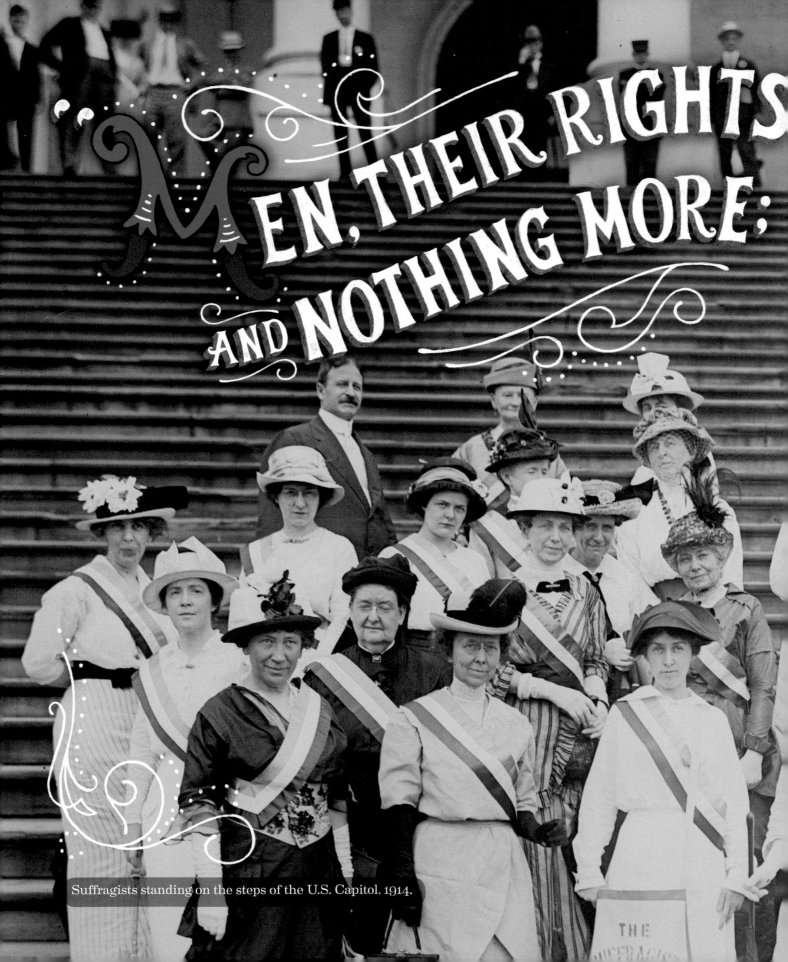

"**MEN, THEIR RIGHTS; AND NOTHING MORE;**

Suffragists standing on the steps of the U.S. Capitol, 1914.

Imagine that you are a woman living in the United States in the early 1800s.

You probably don't work outside the home, but if you do, and you are married, your husband has the right to take your pay. Did your parents or relatives leave you an inheritance? Sorry—that automatically becomes your husband's property.

Not married? Well, you might get to keep your own money . . . but you'll have a hard time earning any. There are only a few jobs open to women. You can be a teacher, perhaps, or a seamstress. And with no husband and no children to take care of, many people will look down on you. You'll be called an "old maid."

Oh, and one more thing. You will not be able to vote.

That's right. Until 1920, there was no national law that guaranteed all women in the United States the right to vote.

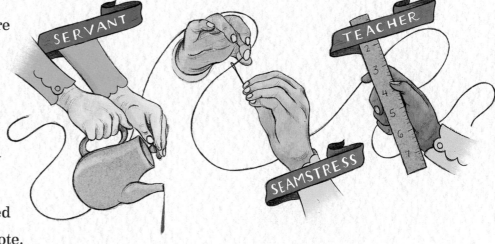

Who decided women couldn't vote? It's easy to blame it on the men. From the pulpit, preachers taught that females were inferior to males. Not many fathers wanted to see their daughters educated or, worse, hold jobs. It wasn't considered ladylike. But the idea of voting seemed strange to women, too. And it wasn't just in the United States that women couldn't vote. Until the 1860s, there was hardly any place in the world where a woman could cast a vote.

It took a lot of work and a lot of time and a lot of effort to get women in the United States the right to vote. It took women with big ideas, buckets of courage, and plenty of patience.

The U.S. suffrage movement (*suffrage* means the right to vote) started in

1848, when Elizabeth Cady Stanton, Lucretia Mott, and some three hundred others came together at a women's rights convention in Seneca Falls, New York. The conference ended with a declaration that men and women are equal, with equal rights. And one of those was the right to vote.

Stanton and Mott were soon joined by Amelia Bloomer (she, shockingly, wore pant outfits that came to be called "bloomers") and the tireless Susan B. Anthony, who would fight for decades for woman suffrage (and provide the quotation used as the title of this section). Thousands of other women across the country also marched, lobbied, and even went to jail for the vote.

It seemed foolish for women to run for office if they didn't have the right to vote. Who would vote for them? But in the late 1800s, some women in the United States ran anyway.

Victoria Woodhull, the first female stockbroker on Wall Street, and a very successful one at that, ran for the presidency of the United States in 1872 as a candidate from the Equal Rights Party. Many people questioned whether it was even legal for her to run—because she was a woman, because she couldn't vote, because she was not thirty-five years old, the minimum age the Constitution says one must be to be president.

But the colorful Woodhull—who believed in otherworldly spirits, advocated shorter skirts at a time when dresses swept the floor, and refused to be reined in by society's conventions—was determined to make a statement about inequality. She wanted people to think about women's rights. Her candidacy attracted so much attention that she tried again in 1884 and 1892.

Belva Lockwood, an attorney who had to fight for her right to be educated and practice law, made a more serious run for the presidency in 1884. She got about 4,000 votes nationwide, but many of those were simply thrown out by vote counters who didn't think her candidacy was legal. She ran again in 1888.

In 1920, all the hard work paid off! The Nineteenth Amendment to the Constitution was passed:

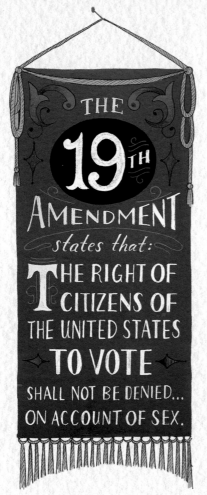

The right of citizens of the United States to vote shall not be denied or abridged by the United States or by any State on account of sex.

At long last, all women across the land had the right to vote. But in some places in the United States, women had received the vote earlier. Out West, pioneer women often faced the same hardships as men and felt they deserved the same rights and privileges. Rugged individualists of both sexes brought the vote to the West while their Eastern sisters still fought to put their check mark on the ballot.

"This shall be the Land for Women!" declared one female journalist about the West, and that turned out to be true. Before the Nineteenth Amendment to the U.S. Constitution was passed, women were voting in territories and states across the West.

Wyoming came first in 1869, four years after the Civil War ended. Wyoming—just a territory, not yet a state—granted full voting rights to women. In 1890, Wyoming entered the Union as the first state whose female citizens were able to vote. A whole crop of Western states followed Wyoming's lead: Colorado, Utah, Idaho, Washington, California, Oregon, Kansas, Arizona, Montana, Nevada, South Dakota, and Oklahoma. *Yee-haw!*

With eyes as wide open as the land they lived on, folks from Montana didn't stop there. In 1916, four years before all the women in the United States got the vote, the citizens of Montana sent the first woman to the U.S. Congress. She was well educated and well traveled, hated war, and was passionate about peace. Her name was Jeannette Rankin.

Born in 1880, Jeannette Rankin grew up near Missoula, riding horses in the shadow of the Montana mountains, under a big sky. The daughter of a rancher and a schoolteacher, the oldest of seven children, she had a mind of her own and the courage to forge her own path.

Jeannette was the kind of girl who stood right up to a challenge. When she was twelve years old, a bloodied horse came galloping onto the Rankin ranch, injured by a run-in with a patch of barbed wire. Jeannette didn't hesitate. She grabbed some hot water and a needle and thread, and while a couple of the ranch hands held down the injured animal, she sewed up the wound.

As an adult, Jeannette Rankin also saw what needed to be fixed and did her level best to try to fix it. Unwilling to be harnessed by conventions like marriage and family, she had the time and energy to take up the cause of immigrants and their dismal living conditions. In the early 1900s, Rankin went first to San Francisco and then to New York, where she attended classes in social work and helped the immigrant families—Irish, Italian, Jewish—flooding the two cities.

But Rankin came to realize that there might be a better way to help the poor, hungry, and underrepresented of the country. New laws were needed—laws that would open up possibilities for people. And

JEANNETTE RANKIN

who better to help pass those laws than women struggling to raise families in difficult circumstances?

If only women could vote.

In 1910, Rankin was in Seattle, Washington. The question of women's voting rights was on the Washington ballot. Jeannette walked into a woman suffrage office, where volunteers were needed to work for passage of a state referendum on the issue. She said she'd do whatever she could, and she found out that what she did best was talk. Traveling around the state, Rankin spoke in halls and on street corners, drumming up support for woman suffrage. In 1910, the men of Washington cast their ballots, and when the votes were counted, the women of Washington came up winners. They were now allowed to vote in the state.

After that, Jeannette Rankin went from coast to coast fighting for the vote. Then she went back home to help with the battle there. It was her ringing speeches in 1914 that helped women get the vote in Montana. Now she was ready to take the next step. She was going to run for a seat in the United States Congress, to be one of the two representatives from her home state.

Some people thought she was crazy. Some people, including many of her supporters, believed in her cause but didn't think she could win. She proved the doubters wrong. On November 6, 1916, in Missoula, Montana, Jeannette Rankin proudly voted for herself. The next day she learned she had won her race. "I may be the first woman member of Congress," she declared, "but I won't be the last."

Rankin's entrance to the House of Representatives in Washington, D.C., was dramatic. On March 5, 1917, she, along with the male members of the 65th Congress, took their oath of office. She was the first representative in U.S. history to be called "congresswoman." When Jeannette Rankin marched into the House, the members rose and cheered.

But her arrival was dramatic for another important reason. The United States Congress was about to vote on going to war.

The question of whether to enter World War I had split the nation. War had broken out in Europe in 1914. Millions were dying. On the very day Jeannette Rankin entered the House of Representatives, President Woodrow Wilson asked for a vote allowing the United States to join Great Britain and France in their fight against Germany.

Jeannette was a pacifist. She did not believe in war. She had told voters during the campaign that if there was going to be a war, they ought to send the old men and leave the young men at home. But when Congress debated entering the war, she listened. She heard from her supporters back home, too. Some wanted her to stick to her pacifist views. Some wanted her to vote for war. They didn't want her to look weak on her first vote.

In the end, she held to her beliefs. A few days after she entered the halls of Congress, she voted nay, or no. "I want to stand by my country, but I cannot vote for war."

The vote was 374 for entering the war, 50 against. The newspaper in Helena, Montana, called Rankin "a crying schoolgirl."

Before her congressional career had barely started, Rankin sealed her fate. She came to understand she would probably not be reelected to Congress. Her vote was unpopular across the country and at home in Montana. Still, she had two years to serve. During that time she worked on women's issues, co-sponsoring a health bill for women and children, and she spoke strongly when the House debated the constitutional amendment that would grant women across the country the right to vote.

Rankin also stood up against the powerful Anaconda Mining Company in Montana, fighting for the miners who were trying to form a union. Nor did she turn her back on the soldiers. She may not have liked the war, but she voted for many military bills because she wanted those fighting to be safe, and she wanted the war to be won as quickly as possible.

Despite the unpopularity of her war vote, Rankin was no quitter. She ran again in 1918, this time for the U.S. Senate, but Montana voters said "No thanks" to her candidacy. What would she do now?

Well, she didn't stop fighting for the causes she believed in. She saw the Nineteenth Amendment to the Constitution enacted, so that women everywhere in the United States could vote. She fought for the rights of mothers and children to have good health care. She made time for her friends and family, and though she lived in different places, she was always drawn back to big sky country, her Montana home.

But most of all, she championed peace. For ten years starting in 1929, she worked for the National Council for Prevention of War. Events in Europe, however, were spiraling out of control. By 1939, Adolf Hitler and his Nazi party had seized power in Germany and were invading other European countries. Another terrifying war had begun. Many Americans wanted to stay out of it.

With the United States still trying to make its way out of the Great Depression, with 20 percent of the population unemployed and war raging across the Atlantic, Jeannette Rankin returned to Montana and, at sixty years of age, ran once more for Congress. She told the citizens of Montana, "By voting for me . . . you can express your opposition to sending your son to foreign lands to fight in a foreign war." They agreed, and in November 1940, Rankin was sent back to the U.S. House of Representatives.

During 1941, Rankin worked on legislation to keep the United States out of war. Then, shockingly, on December 7, Japan, one of Germany's allies, attacked Pearl Harbor in Hawaii. More than two thousand servicepeople died. President Franklin Delano Roosevelt told the country that the attack was "a day which will live in infamy." On December 8, the president asked Congress to declare war.

Many members in the House and Senate had been against the United States entering the war, but the brutal attack changed their minds. Only one person voted against the declaration of war, and that person was Jeannette Rankin.

"No! As a woman I cannot go to war, and I refuse to send anyone else."

After this vote, everyone turned against her. She received hate mail from across Montana and across the country. Still, she could bear, as she put it, "to be a worm." She would not compromise her belief: "We are all human beings and we have to live on this earth and we have to find a way of settling our disputes without force and violence."

When her term was up in 1942, Rankin knew she would not be reelected. Instead, she spent the rest of her life trying to put her ideals into effect. On January 15, 1968, at the age of eighty-seven, Jeannette Rankin led five thousand women through the streets of Washington, D.C., to her old workplace, the Capitol Building. The marchers were protesting the war in Vietnam.

Whatever the consequences, to herself or her career, she never stopped fighting for what she believed in—and what Jeannette Rankin believed in most was peace. "Peace," she said, "is a woman's job."

The second woman to serve in the U.S. House of Representatives came off the prairie. Like Jeannette Rankin, Alice Mary Robertson grew up in wide spaces under an open sky, but there were big differences between them. The biggest? Robertson was only a lukewarm supporter of a woman's right to vote. And while Rankin was a pacifist, Robertson had helped recruit soldiers for Teddy Roosevelt's Rough Riders, the U.S. cavalry that served during the 1898 Spanish-American War.

Alice Mary Robertson was born and raised in territory that belonged to the Creek Indians, before it became the state of Oklahoma. Her parents were missionaries, and they translated many books, including the Bible, into the Creek language. After graduating from college in New York, Robertson worked at the Bureau of Indian Affairs of the Department of the Interior in Washington, D.C.

Miss Alice, as she came to be called, returned to Oklahoma in 1880. Her passion was teaching, and Native Americans were her students. She also ran the post office in the town of Muskogee. But she was best known around Oklahoma as a farmer and the owner of Muskogee's Sawokla Café. *Sawokla* means "gathering place" in the Creek language, and people sure did gather: local folk and their politicians came to have a cup of coffee and a piece of Miss Alice's cake, and to talk, talk, talk.

What Miss Alice was not was a feminist—a person who champions women's rights. Women, she believed, were better off being treated as ladies by their menfolk, who were supposed to protect and financially support them. She particularly didn't like the leaders

ALICE MARY ROBERTSON

of national women's groups and thought modern women were "bartering the birthright for a mess of pottage." That meant women would be giving up a lot if they played a larger role in society and not getting much in return.

Her dim view of women's rights, however, didn't stop her from throwing her hat into the political ring. In 1920—at the age of sixty-six—Miss Alice ran for a seat in the U.S. House as a Republican, challenging a three-term Democrat who held the congressional seat in eastern Oklahoma. Her opponent was a lawyer, and Robertson said there were enough lawyers in Congress. "The farmers need a farmer, I am a farmer. The women need a woman to look after their new responsibilities. The soldier boys need a proven friend."

To get the word out about her campaign, she put ads in the newspaper promoting herself, her candidacy— and her café. She beat her competitor by just 228 votes out of the 50,000 cast. When she got to Washington in 1921, she was the only woman in the entire 67th Congress.

Always dressed in black, Miss Alice spent her two years in Congress fighting for Native American welfare bills. They never got put to a vote. That made her mad. She voted against a bill aimed at helping mothers and infants. That made women's groups mad. And surprisingly, even though she was a supporter of the armed services, she voted against a bill that would have allowed World War I veterans to receive an early payment on their pensions. That made the vets mad, despite her support of other legislation that would help them, including a hospital in her hometown.

In 1921, Alice Mary Robertson, gavel in hand, was the first woman to preside over a session of the U.S. Congress (the responsibility of presiding over a congressional session is given to junior members of the majority party on a rotating basis). Robertson ran for reelection the next year but lost her bid for another term. She went home to Muskogee. In 1931, she died at the veterans' hospital she helped bring to her district.

Campers at the Federal Emergency Relief Administration (FERA) camp for unemployed women in Arcola, Pennsylvania. FERA created jobs for unemployed men and women.

FLASH and CRASH

1920-1930

orld War I ended in 1918. By 1920, the United States was turning into a very different country from what it had been before the war. An economy based on land and farming was becoming more industrialized, and people were moving to cities to take advantage of the ever-increasing jobs. There was a sense of "out with the old and in with the new."

Now you could listen to music, sports, and news on an invention called radio. And movies, which had been silent until the 1920s, got sound. Talkies! Women's long skirts became shorter, brushing their knees, and their hairdos got shorter too, scandalizing many. Men who had fought overseas during the war had been changed by their experiences and weren't always willing to go back to their prewar lives. There was even a popular song about it: "How You Gonna Keep 'Em Down on the Farm After They've Seen Paree?" (referring to Paris).

Another big change? Suddenly, there were so many new things to buy! Automobiles, electrical appliances, phonographs, even frozen vegetables—things that hadn't been readily available (some hadn't even been invented) only a decade earlier.

But one of the biggest changes in American life happened due to a revolutionary movement pushed by reformers, many of them women: Prohibition.

On January 17, 1920, the Eighteenth

Amendment to the Constitution went into effect. The amendment banned the manufacture and sale (though not the possession) of intoxicating liquors. The United States became "dry."

People who supported Prohibition thought alcohol led to all sorts of social ills, especially abuse of women and children by drunken men. Some business owners wanted Prohibition because they felt when their employees were drinking, it affected their work.

But there was one big problem with Prohibition, as everyone—those for and those against—soon found out: it couldn't be enforced. Right from the first, liquor was smuggled into the country or produced illegally. Law enforcement couldn't keep up. Things got worse as gangsters like Al Capone saw ways of making lots of money by providing liquor to whoever wanted it.

Prohibition came to be one of the most unpopular laws the United States has ever seen. In 1933, the amendment was repealed. Even most of its supporters realized Prohibition was a failure.

In many ways, the 1920s were a lot like the period before the more recent economic dive of 2008. The stock market was running wild, people were spending money they didn't have, and everyone thought the party would never end. In 1929, it all came tumbling down. The stock market crashed, many people lost their savings, and it was very difficult to find work. The period that followed the "Roaring Twenties" was called the Great Depression.

REBECCA FELTON * WINNIFRED HUCK
MAE NOLAN * KATHERINE LANGLEY
FLORENCE KAHN * MARY NORTON
EDITH ROGERS

Almost every woman who followed Jeannette Rankin and Alice Mary Robertson to Washington in the 1920s got there because of connections to the men in their lives. Some were appointed to finish their late husbands' or fathers' terms in office. Some went on to win new elections on their own once the men's terms were up. Some stayed in Congress for decades. One left after only a day.

That woman was Rebecca Felton. She was the United States' first woman senator—even if it was for only twenty-four hours. Why so short? Felton was an active partner in her husband's political career. She was his campaign manager when he ran as a Democrat and won a seat in the U.S. Congress from Georgia in 1875: "I made appointments for speaking, recruited speakers, answered newspaper attacks. . . ." A talented writer who could turn out everything from homey newspaper columns to books on Georgia politics, she also wrote lots of her husband's speeches. People said that by voting for William Felton, they were getting two representatives for the price of one.

After her husband's death in 1909, Mrs. Felton stayed active in politics, fighting for causes she believed in, such as giving women the vote and funding education for girls. Unfortunately, her views on race weren't nearly so progressive. Her tirades against black men were sharp and highly offensive, especially by today's standards. She railed against anyone who questioned segregation.

Then, when she was eighty-seven years old, Rebecca Felton got the call. That's right, eighty-seven! In 1922, one of Georgia's senators died. The Democratic governor, Thomas Hardwick, wanted that seat for himself, but he needed someone to sit in it until there could be a special election. Someone who didn't have notions about running.

Plenty of Georgia's women were angry at Hardwick for opposing their right to vote before the passage of the Nineteenth Amendment. So the governor thought he might pick up support by appointing Rebecca Felton, who was known across the state for her popular newspaper column. She went to Washington, and on November 21, 1922, at twelve o'clock noon, she was sworn into the United States Senate.

REBECCA FELTON

The event was more symbolism than substance. She had been appointed in October, but Congress wasn't in session. The special election for the Senate seat was held later that month, and Governor Hardwick lost. When President Woodrow Wilson called Congress into session unexpectedly in November, Mrs. Felton went to Washington for her swearing in, knowing she would resign a day later and let the winner of the special election take the seat.

In her only congressional speech, she had something to say about the women who would follow her into the Senate: "I pledge you that you will get ability, you will get integrity of purpose, you will get exalted patriotism, and you will get unstinted usefulness." Then the United States' first woman senator packed up and went home to Georgia, where she lived until the ripe old age of ninety-four.

* * * * * * *

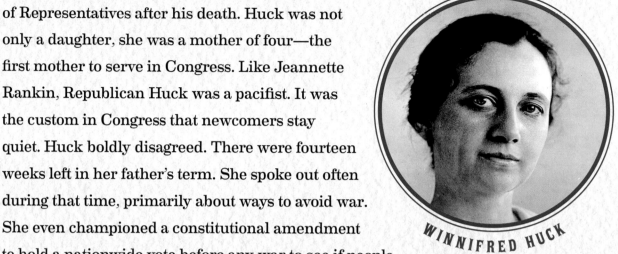

The trend of women taking their husbands' or fathers' seats in Congress continued in 1922. That year Winnifred Huck from Illinois decided to run in a special election for her father's seat in the House of Representatives after his death. Huck was not only a daughter, she was a mother of four—the first mother to serve in Congress. Like Jeannette Rankin, Republican Huck was a pacifist. It was the custom in Congress that newcomers stay quiet. Huck boldly disagreed. There were fourteen weeks left in her father's term. She spoke out often during that time, primarily about ways to avoid war. She even championed a constitutional amendment to hold a nationwide vote before any war to see if people really wanted to fight overseas. It never passed, but the United States has been in several unpopular wars since then: Korea, Vietnam, Iraq. Who knows what would have happened if the country could have voted to stay out or get in?

WINNIFRED HUCK

✳ ✳ ✳ ✳ ✳ ✳

Mae Nolan and Florence Kahn had a lot in common. Both were from San Francisco, California. They were both members of minority groups: Nolan was Catholic, the daughter of Irish immigrants. Kahn was Jewish, the daughter of Polish immigrants. And both came to Congress as widows filling the seats of their late husbands, Republican representatives. Nolan arrived first, in 1923. Kahn followed in 1925. Both women won special elections to claim their seats.

MAE NOLAN

While Mae Nolan was in Congress, she mostly carried on with her husband's work. His issues were ones that she also strongly believed in: fighting for children's welfare and education and making sure people could earn a decent wage. She was the first woman to chair a congressional committee, one of the small groups within Congress that work to get laws studied and passed.

In 1925, Nolan decided she would not run again. She wanted to return to California, where she could focus on raising her daughter. She wouldn't miss the attention she got from the press—some reporters had made fun of her round figure and laughed at the way she took up golf for exercise.

Even though Nolan had many friends in Congress, having worked alongside her husband, she had found politics to be a very frustrating profession. She came away from her time in Washington believing "A capable woman is a better representative than an incapable man, and vice versa."

Mae Nolan's friend Florence Kahn didn't go home. She stayed in the House of Representatives for twelve years.

Florence was a graduate of the University of California at Berkeley at a time when most young women didn't go to college. She wanted to continue on to law school, but her family needed financial help, so she became a teacher.

FLORENCE KAHN

In 1899, Florence married Julius Kahn, a Republican representative to the U.S. House from San Francisco, and for twenty-five years she supported him in his work. When Julius died in 1924, local Republicans asked her to run in the special election for his seat. She won, beating out three opponents, and became the first Jewish woman to serve in Congress.

Having been her husband's political aide, Florence knew the inner workings of the House. She made sure the committees she served on were the important ones. In her second term, she joined the Military Affairs Committee. In 1933, she won a chair on the most influential committee of all, Appropriations—it decides where the government's money gets spent.

Kahn saw to it that a lot of money got spent in her district of San Francisco. She helped make sure naval installations were built in the Bay Area, and she was a driving force behind the construction of the Golden Gate Bridge and the San Francisco–Bay Bridge. Her voters liked that.

She strongly supported law enforcement. J. Edgar Hoover, the first director of the Federal Bureau of Investigation, created in 1935, called her the "mother of the F.B.I."

A popular member of Congress, she was said to be feared, admired, listened to, and treated "like a man."

Florence Kahn also had a sharp sense of humor. When someone once asked her how she managed to be such a successful congresswoman, she stood there in her shapeless black dress, tight tiny curls, and pince-nez glasses and answered, "Sex appeal!"

Alice Roosevelt Longworth, the oldest daughter of President Theodore Roosevelt and a smart, sharp woman in her own right, said it best: "Mrs. Kahn, shrewd, resourceful, and witty, is an all around first-rate legislator, the equal of any man in Congress and the superior of most."

* * * * * * *

Three more women came to the House of Representatives in the late 1920s. Two of them, Pearl Oldfield (see page 34) from Arkansas and Katherine Langley of Kentucky, served only short terms. Edith Nourse Rogers, who hailed from Massachusetts, the first congresswoman from New

KATHERINE LANGLEY

EDITH ROGERS

England, arrived in 1925, and she didn't leave until she died in 1960. Thirty-five years in Congress! Eighteen consecutive terms! She held the record as the woman to serve the longest in Congress until 2012, when that distinction was taken by Senator Barbara Mikulski of Maryland.

Like Florence Kahn, Edith Rogers had been her husband's close adviser. John and Edith Rogers were an influential Washington, D.C., couple. When Representative Rogers died of cancer, Edith decided immediately to run for his seat. She won the special election with 72 percent of the vote.

For thirty-five years, Republican Edith Rogers spoke up. She was one of the first in Congress during the 1930s to warn about Adolf Hitler and his persecution of the Jews. She fought for the right of women to serve in the armed forces. She championed war veterans. And everyone always knew her when she walked down the halls of Congress because of the big, bright flower she had pinned to her shoulder.

* * * * * *

There was one woman who came to Congress in the 1920s on her own. She was the politician in the family—not her father, not her husband.

Mary Norton was the first female Democrat elected to Congress. All the rest of them, from Rankin

MARY NORTON

and Robertson all the way to Rogers, were Republicans. (Rebecca Felton was a Democrat, but she was appointed, not elected.)

Mary Norton, who was from New Jersey, won her race for the House of Representatives in 1924. A newspaper reporter thought she'd be a good human interest story and asked her to pose for some photographs—one in the kitchen and another hanging up the laundry. She glared at him. "I do not expect to cook, and I do not expect to wash any clothes in Congress!"

In her twenty-five years in the House of Representatives, Norton led the fight for a better life for America's working class. So hard did she charge that folks called her "Battling Mary." She pushed for safer working conditions, a higher minimum wage, and a forty-hour workweek. She successfully shepherded the Fair Labor Standards Act through Congress in 1938, establishing a national minimum wage, guaranteeing extra money for working overtime, and prohibiting most employment for minors. Norton said, "I'm prouder of getting that bill through the House than anything I've done in my life."

Mary Norton left the House of Representatives in 1951. She had served through America's Great Depression and World War II, but she is probably best remembered for something she said during her very first term. When one of her fellow congressmembers offered to let her speak first because she was a lady, she tartly replied, "I am no lady, I'm a Member of Congress!"

CHAPTER 4
...AND DAUGHTERS

RUTH HANNA McCORMICK
RUTH BRYAN OWEN

Two women came to the U.S. House of Representatives in 1929, the year the stock market crashed and America fell into the Great Depression. One was a Republican, one a Democrat. They both became interested in politics because of their fathers—powerful, important men. But these daughters, both named Ruth, proved that they, too, could play in the big leagues.

* * * * * *

Ruth Hanna grew up as the daughter of a political "kingmaker." Her father, Mark Hanna, was the mastermind behind Republican William McKinley's successful bid for the presidency in 1896. Soon Hanna had his own career as one of the two U.S. senators from Ohio, and he wielded great power. Ruth traveled with her father and became his personal aide when he went to Washington. She must have been paying attention, because politics became a passion of hers, too.

In 1903, Ruth Hanna married Joseph Medill McCormick, who was part of the newspaper family that owned the influential *Chicago Tribune*. Mr. McCormick

Ruth, THERE ARE 2 THINGS THAT ARE IMPORTANT IN POLITICS. THE FIRST IS MONEY AND I CAN'T REMEMBER THE SECOND.

RUTH HANNA McCORMICK

got into politics, winning his election to become a member of the Illinois legislature; at the same time, his wife worked hard to pass the Illinois Municipal Voting Act of 1913. Mr. McCormick went on to higher office, first as a member of the U.S. House in 1916; in 1918, he ran for and won a Senate seat. Ruth McCormick was forging her own political future, organizing women from around Illinois into Republican women's clubs. She knew if and when she decided to run for office, they'd be there to help.

By 1928, Ruth McCormick had been a widow for several years. It was time to take the plunge and run for office. Hoping to win a seat in the U.S. House of Representatives from Illinois, she promoted herself as an experienced politician. Calling on her experience with her powerful father, she said, "I have been a political worker for more years than most of the men in the party today." She won. Even though she said she wasn't running as a woman, her high visibility among the women of Illinois pushed her into office.

Now Ruth Hanna McCormick had her seat in Congress. But she had her eye on a bigger prize. She wasn't content to be a representative. Like her late husband, she wanted to be a senator.

The Republican Party backed McCormick. But an independent Republican in the race—another woman—took away a number of votes Ruth would otherwise have gotten. McCormick had other problems as well. It was 1930, the effects of the Depression were hurting the country, and many people had lost their jobs. So the voters of Illinois didn't take too kindly to learning McCormick had spent hundreds of thousands of dollars on her campaign. She tried to defend the spending as necessary, but the voters weren't buying. She lost her Senate race, and her political career was over.

Maybe she had learned one lesson from her father too well. Mark Hanna was remembered for saying, "There are two things that are important in politics. The first is money and I can't remember the second."

* * * * * *

Ruth Hanna McCormick's father may have been powerful, but Ruth Bryan Owen's father was one of the most popular politicians in the country. William Jennings Bryan was elected to the U.S. House of Representatives when Ruth was five, but he was best known for his three runs at the presidency.

Bryan was a great orator. That means people came from miles around to hear him speak. He gave *loooong* speeches, sometimes four hours long, but folks liked listening to what he had to say. William Jennings Bryan was a liberal Democrat who was for the common man, not the privileged. He was religious as well, and he didn't think those common men (and women) had descended from monkeys. He was firmly against the theory of evolution, believing God had created humans as reported in the Bible.

His powerful public speaking at the 1896 Democratic convention got Bryan his first nomination for the presidency. He was only thirty-six years old! That made him the youngest person to ever run for president. (He was also the first presidential candidate to ever campaign in an automobile.) He lost to Senator Mark Hanna's candidate, William McKinley. In 1900, Bryan ran again. He lost again to McKinley. In 1908, the Democrats gave him the nomination once more. This time, he lost to Republican William Howard Taft.

You might think all this losing would have discouraged Bryan's daughter Ruth from going into politics. But she had been around politics since she was a girl. When her father was a U.S. representative, she played on the House floor and was dubbed "the Sweetheart of the House."

◄ **25** ►

When she grew up, Ruth married, divorced and remarried, and had four children, two from each marriage. At thirty-three years old, now a widow, she decided to take her own chance at elective office.

After losing an election in 1926 for the U.S. House seat of a district that ran along the Florida coast from Jacksonville down to Key West, she tried again as the Democratic candidate in 1928. Like her father, Ruth hopped into a car to campaign. She dubbed it "the Spirit of Florida" and drove it up and down the coast, traveling 10,000 miles. And like her father, Ruth Bryan Owen was a darn good speaker; she seemed to understand the voters' needs. Owen won the 1928 election handily, with 65 percent of the vote.

Despite the win, the battle wasn't quite over. Her Republican opponent contested the election, claiming Owen wasn't a citizen. Even though she was born and raised in the United States, her second marriage had been to a man from England, and she'd lived there for a while. Her challenger claimed that she had forfeited her citizenship because of that. Ruth Owen begged to differ. Had any man ever lost his citizenship because he married a foreign woman? No, he had not! She won the argument and the office.

Owen's biggest success in the House of Representatives came in battling the Mediterranean fruit fly. Yes, it was a little bitty fly, but it caused mighty damage to the Florida citrus crop. Owen obtained $4 million in federal funding to combat the fruit fly. Her constituents liked that. They liked how she fought for the health and welfare of women and children. They liked that she kept an aide in Florida who could tell her what the voters were thinking, which was unusual at the time.

RUTH BRYAN OWEN

What they didn't like was her position on Prohibition. By 1932, most of the people in the United States were against Prohibition. They were tired of being "dry." The people of Florida were tired of being dry, too. Ruth Bryan Owen held firm. She thought Prohibition was a good thing. The voters disagreed. When she lost the Democratic nomination, she said it was because "I did not turn 'wet' fast enough."

Ruth Bryan Owen left the House of Representatives in 1933, but she kept busy. She was appointed by President Franklin Roosevelt as ambassador to Denmark, the first woman to become a diplomatic representative to a foreign country.

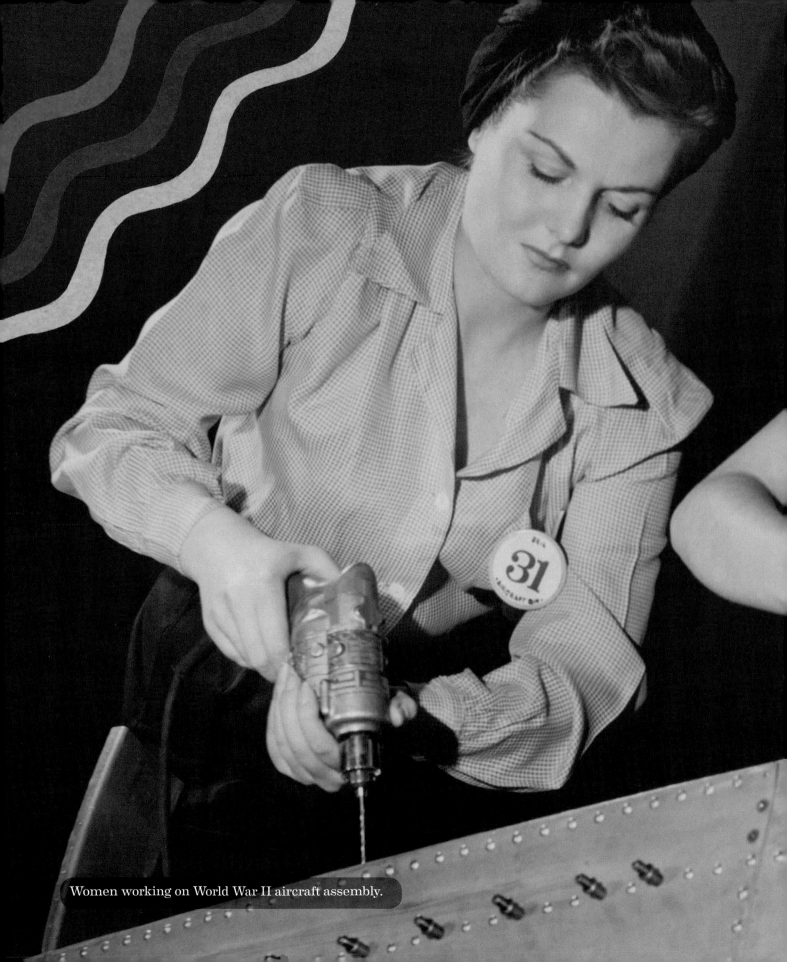

Women working on World War II aircraft assembly.

HARD TIMES

DEPRESSION, WAR, AND THE RED MENACE

1931-1953

In the years from 1917, when Jeannette Rankin entered the House, until 1929, when the financial crash overwhelmed the United States, women had gone to Congress in a trickle. From 1930 until World War II ended in 1945, that trickle . . . remained a trickle.

Oh, women were still arriving in those hallowed halls—a few elected on their own, most appointed to fill their husband's seats—but they made up only a tiny percentage of the U.S. House of Representatives. In the 71st Congress, which spanned the years 1929 to 1931, there were nine woman members in the House of Representatives. Nine women out of 435 representatives. And that was a high point!

Things were even worse in the other half of Congress, the Senate. Most years in the 1930s and '40s, there were no women at all in the ninety-six-member Senate. (There were only forty-eight states back then. Two senators from each state x 48 = 96.) A couple of women came, briefly filled their husband's seats, and then left. Only one, Hattie Caraway of Arkansas, spent a substantial time in the Senate, thirteen years.

The Depression brought a decade of suffering to the United States. By 1933, 25 percent of the country was unemployed. Those who clung to jobs had their wages cut. People couldn't pay their rent and were evicted from their homes. To make a few pennies, both adults and children sold pencils or apples on the street.

With much of the country blaming the Depression on the policies of the Republicans and President Herbert Hoover, the 1932 election brought

Franklin D. Roosevelt to the presidency and his Democratic Party to power. People were looking to the federal government to help them.

Franklin Roosevelt was an optimist, and in his inauguration speech he told the country, "The only thing we have to fear is fear itself." Roosevelt followed his words with actions, pushing through fifteen major bills that would affect every part of the economy during his first one hundred days in office. He laid out what he called a New Deal for the American people. There were programs to help the unemployed, such as the Works Progress Administration (W.P.A.), that created jobs for millions of people. Also, "safety net" programs like Social Security for the elderly were begun. Many people loved Franklin Roosevelt for his efforts; his critics thought Roosevelt had inserted too much federal government into people's lives.

One important thing about Franklin Roosevelt: he recognized the capabilities of women. He appointed one, Frances Perkins, to be his Secretary of Labor, the first female cabinet member in U.S. history. He appointed Ruth Bryan Owen, the former representative from Florida, as the first woman ambassador, and he consulted with woman representatives in Congress, though their number was small. Perhaps most important, his wife, Eleanor Roosevelt, was one of his most valued advisers.

The New Deal did not end the Depression, but it helped. What really ended the Depression was World War II. The war had a strong impact on the economy. The United States needed ships, airplanes, uniforms, and numerous other things necessary for running a war. Now there were more jobs than people to do them, especially when many men— millions—were needed to fight.

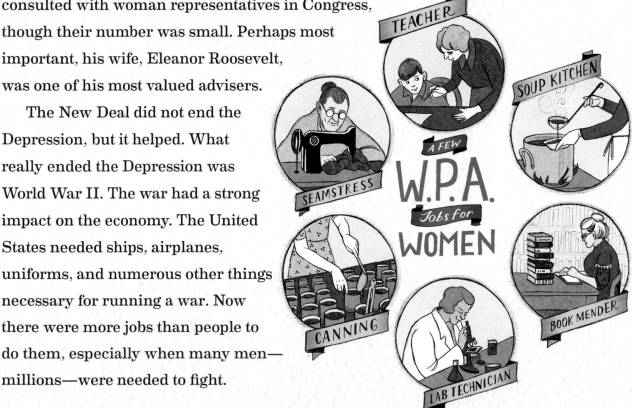

A FEW W.P.A. Jobs for WOMEN

TEACHER

SOUP KITCHEN

SEAMSTRESS

CANNING

LAB TECHNICIAN

BOOK MENDER

World War II brought many American women into the workplace. By taking the jobs left behind by the men who were fighting in Europe and in the Pacific, they helped the war effort and kept the country going. "Rosie the Riveter"—flexing her bicep and saying "We Can Do It!"—was the face of the new American woman.

When World War II came to an end, the United States braced itself for a new threat: the spread of Communism.

During World II, the Union of Soviet Socialist Republics (known as the Soviet Union but often referred to simply as Russia) had been our ally. But after the war was over, Russia began to more aggressively force other countries into their form of political and economic government, Communism. Under Communism, the government owns all the property and distributes goods, unlike in the United States, where ownership is individual. Another big difference between the two systems lay in the rights enjoyed by their citizens. In the U.S. Constitution, Americans are guaranteed important rights, including freedom of speech, freedom of the press, and freedom of religion. Communist governments did not give their citizens any of these.

After World War II, the U.S. government fought a "Cold War" against the Soviet Union. That meant that although the United States and the Soviet Union weren't shooting at each other, they were fighting in many other ways, with spies, with propaganda, and through a nuclear arms race to determine who would have the greatest number of deadly weapons. The Soviet flag was red, and many Americans called the threat of Communism the "Red Menace."

The Great Depression, World War II, the Cold War: though they were few in number, the women of Congress played a role in all these world-shaking events.

CHAPTER 5
THE WOMEN OF ARKANSAS

HATTIE CARAWAY
PEARL OLDFIELD
EFFIEGENE WINGO

During the 1930s and 1940s, at a time when most states didn't have any female members in the U.S. House or Senate, the state of Arkansas had three!

* * * * * *

Hattie Caraway was the second woman to become a senator. Unlike Rebecca Felton of Georgia, who left after twenty-four hours, Hattie Caraway stayed in the Senate for thirteen years.

As with many of the women who came before and after, Hattie's entrée into Congress was the death of her husband, Thaddeus Caraway, the sitting senator from Arkansas. She came to the Senate in 1931, appointed by the governor of Arkansas to fill her husband's seat. When she entered the Senate, her first comment was "The windows need washing!"

With the governor's support, Hattie, a Democrat, next won the special election that would fill her husband's term, another fourteen months. After that, she knew, she would be expected to give up her seat to a male candidate.

But Hattie Caraway decided she didn't want to do that. To the astonishment of the voters, to say nothing of the six men who planned to run for her Senate seat, Caraway announced, "The time has passed when a woman should be placed in a position and kept there only while someone else is being groomed for the job."

HATTIE CARAWAY

Most people didn't give her a ghost of a chance to win.

But Hattie Caraway had a secret weapon. The most popular politician in the South, Huey Long, lived in the state next door, Louisiana. The Kingfish, as he was nicknamed, had been a political ally of Hattie's husband, and now he wanted to extend his influence into Arkansas and thought he could do that by supporting Caraway's candidacy.

The Kingfish was a terrific speechmaker. Hattie Caraway didn't care for public speaking, even though she was a witty woman. When asked why she avoided giving speeches, she once said wryly, "I haven't the heart to take a minute away from the men. The poor dears love it so." She traveled throughout Arkansas with Huey Long, and more than 200,000 people came out to see them. First Hattie won her primary, whupping her male rivals, and then she went on to win the general election.

During her time in the Senate, Caraway was a strong supporter of President Franklin Roosevelt and his New Deal. His programs helped her state with farm relief and flood control. She also knew that the key to reelection was listening to what her voters had to say, and she listened closely from 1931 to 1945.

Hattie Caraway was the first woman, gavel in hand, to ever preside over a session of the Senate.

* * * * * *

Hattie Caraway's first term overlapped with those of two other women from Arkansas. The previously mentioned Pearl Oldfield, a House representative who took office in 1928, was leaving in 1931, just as Caraway was arriving. Oldfield had been living in Washington, D.C., with her husband, William, who was a powerful Arkansas representative in the House. When he died suddenly after complications from gallbladder surgery, party leaders asked that Pearl be appointed to his seat. She was just supposed to finish up the four months left on his term, but she ran and was elected to her own two-year term. That gave her the distinction of being the first woman from the South to be elected—not just appointed—to the House of Representatives.

Miss Pearl, as she was called, used her time in the House to fight for the people she represented in rural Arkansas, who had been hit hard by drought and the Depression. When her term was up, she decided not to run again, but she stayed in Washington, working for children's charities.

PEARL OLDFIELD

* * * * * * *

Effiegene Wingo was also appointed to fill her husband's term, in 1930. She spent several years in the House and, like Pearl Oldfield, used her time to help the people of her state, who were fighting the effects of natural disasters and trying to cope with the economic hardships of the Depression. Because she had worked so closely with her husband when he was a representative, she knew her way around the House and was able to steer many federal projects to her state, bringing in jobs and money. When she left Congress in 1933 for health reasons, Wingo said about her public service that it had been a "sweet privilege to serve my people."

Arkansas had gotten itself off to a good start with its female representation. Unfortunately, it wouldn't be until 1961 that the voters of Arkansas elected another woman to Congress.

EFFIEGENE WINGO

CHAPTER 6

STARS!

MARGARET CHASE SMITH
CLARE BOOTHE LUCE
HELEN GAHAGAN DOUGLAS

Three women you might call "stars" went to Congress in the 1940s. They certainly stood out from the pack.

Margaret Chase Smith became a star because of her many years in both the House and Senate, her dedication to her job, and her bravery in standing up for what she believed in. Clare Boothe Luce and Helen Gahagan Douglas were stars in their own right before they ran for office. Luce was a Broadway playwright and internationally known journalist. Douglas was an actress, married to a movie star.

* * * * * *

Margaret Chase Smith first came to the U.S. House of Representatives as a Republican from the state of Maine in 1940. In 1948, she won a tough election to take a seat in the Senate. All told, she was in Congress for thirty-two years, and throughout her long career, she served as a role model for future legislators. Gutsy, smart, and willing to take a stand: that was Margaret Chase Smith.

Who would have thought that a young Margaret Chase would grow up to serve in Congress?

Probably no one.

She was born in Skowhegan, Maine, and her family was poor. Her father, a barber, drank too much, and her mother worked several jobs to keep the family going. Margaret worked, too. Her first job, at age thirteen, was at the five-and-dime store, where you could buy everything from candy and comic books to lampshades and socks. She would have liked to attend college, but there was no money for it. Instead, she went to work full-time.

Briefly, Margaret taught in a one-room schoolhouse, and she worked in the offices of a local newspaper and a textile mill. Her favorite job was working as a telephone operator. An older gentleman would often call to get the correct time. (You could do that in those days.) He and Margaret got to talking. And talking. Then they started dating. They dated a long time. Ten years! Finally, in 1930, Margaret Chase, thirty-two, married fifty-three-year-old Clyde Smith.

Clyde had political ambitions. He was elected as a Republican to the House of Representatives in 1936. Margaret enjoyed living in Washington, D.C. It was quite a change from small-town Maine. She managed her husband's office, joined an organization for House members' wives, and got to meet the first lady of the United States, Eleanor Roosevelt.

Then, in 1940, Clyde Smith fell ill; before he died, he asked his wife to run for his seat in the House. She agreed and won. So began Margaret Chase Smith's amazing congressional career.

With World War II on the horizon, Representative Smith worked hard on the Naval Affairs and Armed Services Committees. She learned a lot, and military affairs became one of her passions. She fought to make sure that army and navy nurses, almost all women at the time, would no longer be considered volunteers and would receive benefits just the way male members of the armed services did.

Then, in 1947, one of Maine's two Senate seats came open. Margaret Chase Smith decided that she would like to go from the House into the Senate, and she became one of a crowd of candidates vying for the Republican nomination.

Maine's population is small, and that enabled Smith to travel around the state meeting many of the residents personally. People felt as if they knew her, and some just called her by her first name. After months of campaigning, she won the Senate seat. Seventy-one percent of the voters in Maine cast their

MARGARET CHASE SMITH

ballots for Margaret Chase Smith. She was the first woman to win a Senate seat without being appointed or having a husband sitting in it first.

By now, World War II was over, but the country was worried about something else: the spread of Communism. America's former ally, the Soviet Union, was now its enemy, and the question that plagued U.S. leaders was whether countries around the world were going to be democracies, like the United States, or become Communist, like the Soviets. There were a number of people in the United States who hated and feared the Soviet Union. One of the people who played on those emotions was a senator from the state of Wisconsin, Joseph McCarthy.

Senator McCarthy claimed there were Communists working throughout the U.S. government. He began making accusations against people, who then lost their jobs and their reputations. Many had done nothing wrong, but the more Senator McCarthy spoke, the more powerful he became. People feared him. They were afraid to stand up to him, to insist that much of what he was saying was not true, because then Senator McCarthy might come after them.

Enter Senator Smith. On June 1, 1950, Senator McCarthy asked Margaret Chase Smith on the floor of the Senate if she was going to make a speech about him. He had heard rumors to that effect. She said she was, adding, "And you're not going to like it."

Smith then stood up to make what she called a "Declaration of Conscience." She accused Joe McCarthy of "selfish political exploitation of fear, bigotry, ignorance, and intolerance." She said, "The American people are sick and tired of being afraid to speak their minds lest they be politically smeared as 'Communists.'"

THE AMERICAN·PEOPLE ARE SICK AND TIRED OF BEING AFRAID TO SPEAK THEIR MINDS.

Her speech didn't stop Senator McCarthy, but Smith had taken a brave stand, and a good chunk of the country appreciated that. It wasn't until four years later, in 1954, that the Senate told Senator McCarthy he had gone too far and condemned his actions.

In 1964, Senator Margaret Chase Smith made another speech. It began with a list of reasons why she shouldn't run for the office of president of the United States, including the fact that no one thought she could win. Then she said she was running anyway. "When people keep telling you, you can't do a thing, you kind of like to try."

She didn't win. But she had added to her list of "firsts": first woman to run for president from a major political party.

Despite being a Republican, Senator Smith had the heart of a maverick, sometimes voting against the policies of Republican presidents Dwight D. Eisenhower, and later, Richard M. Nixon. After thirty-two years in Congress, and a run of 2,941 consecutive votes (1955 to 1968, broken only by her hip surgery), seventy-year-old Margaret Chase Smith lost her Senate seat in 1972 to her Democratic challenger.

But honors were still to come to this trailblazer. In 1989, President George H. W. Bush awarded her the Presidential Medal of Freedom. The medal recognizes men and women who have made special contributions to the United States.

It is the nation's highest civilian honor.

* * * * * * *

Bright, beautiful, a successful playwright, an intrepid foreign correspondent—Clare Boothe Luce was all of these before she was ever elected to the House of Representatives as a Republican from the state of Connecticut. But, as with Margaret Chase Smith, the future hadn't seemed very bright for young Clare.

Clare's parents weren't married, and by the time she was eight, they had gone their separate ways. It wasn't an easy childhood, but her mother, who was

CLARE BOOTHE LUCE

a dancer, did get Clare on the stage as an understudy. That experience fueled a passion in the girl. She wanted to become an actress.

Instead, at age twenty, she became a wife, and a year later the mother of a daughter, Ann. Her first marriage didn't work out; then, when Clare was thirty-two, she married a man who was rich and powerful. Henry Luce made his fortune in publishing a host of magazines Americans wanted to read: *Time* reported the week's news; *Life* was a photo essay of how Americans lived; *Fortune*, well, that was about business and money. But Clare Boothe didn't need Henry Luce for her success. She had already written several popular plays, including *The Women*, and was the editor of the magazine *Vanity Fair* by the time they married.

Marriage to Luce did open one new career for Clare, however: war correspondent. She went overseas before and during World War II to report on the fighting. She traveled to Europe, Africa, India, China, Burma, often at great risk to herself. A woman noted for her perceptive way with words, she had this to say about war: "[M]en have decided to die together because they are unable to find a way to live together."

Her experience as a national and international observer encouraged Republicans to recruit her for a House run from the state of

Connecticut. At first Clare declined, mainly because she didn't care much about politics. But she did care about winning the war and having an enduring peace afterward, so she stood for election and won.

Luce was a smart and witty speaker, and Republicans liked her for the very reason that Democrats didn't: she was an effective voice against President Franklin Roosevelt. Her efforts against Communism and her role in establishing the Atomic Energy Commission, created by Congress to help control the development of atomic science and technology, were her main issues during her time in Congress.

Then, in 1944, Luce's daughter Ann died in a car crash, and she decided not to run for elective office again. She went on to write several more plays and movies. President Dwight Eisenhower appointed her to serve as ambassador to Italy from 1953 to 1957. In 1983, President Ronald Reagan bestowed upon Clare Boothe Luce the Presidential Medal of Freedom.

When she died in 1989, the *Washington Post* said in her obituary, "She raised early feminist hell. . . . Unlike so many . . . Washingtonians, she was neither fearful nor ashamed of what she meant to say."

＊ ＊ ＊ ＊ ＊ ＊ ＊

Helen Gahagan Douglas was an actress and a singer, but she was more than just a pretty face. Once she entered Congress as a Democrat from California, she would be a passionate advocate for causes she believed in, especially equal rights for women and African Americans.

HELEN GAHAGAN DOUGLAS

Helen Gahagan had some of the best schooling a girl in America could get. Her college, Barnard, was in New York City. But instead of studying, she was dazzled by the bright lights of Broadway. She dropped out of school—against her well-to-do father's wishes—and went onstage, acting and singing. It was during the run of the 1930 hit play *Tonight or Never* that she married her costar, Melvyn Douglas. Together they moved out to California to try their luck in movies.

Melvyn Douglas did become a well-respected movie actor, but Helen, after only one movie, turned her attention to other, more important things. "I became active in politics because I saw the possibility, if we all sat back and did nothing, of a world in which there would no longer be any stages for actors to act on."

Helen Gahagan Douglas saw with her own eyes a lot of what worried her. When traveling to California during the early days of the Depression, she had witnessed the plight of migrant workers, their low pay and difficult working conditions. With her husband, she went to Europe and Japan in the 1930s and saw that war was brewing and intolerance was on the march. She supported President Franklin Roosevelt's policies as he tried to lift the country out of the Great Depression, and she became friends with his wife, Eleanor, a powerhouse in her own right.

Helen believed in the liberal ideals of the Democratic Party: civil rights, labor rights, and playing an active part in international relations. She decided to run for Congress in 1944. First, she beat out seven male candidates to win the Democratic nomination. Then in the general election, she narrowly beat the Republican candidate. Her view of politics was simple: "Politics is a job that needs doing—by anyone who is interested enough to train for it and work at it. It's like housekeeping; someone has to do it. Whether the job is done by men or women is not important—only whether the job is done well or badly."

Representative Douglas, with her experience on the stage, was a polished speaker. In her spare time, she traveled across the country addressing the issues she believed in. One of those issues was equality for African American citizens. Much of the United States was segregated: black Americans couldn't attend the same schools, pursue equal housing and employment, or even eat in the same places, drink from the same water fountains, or use the same bathrooms as white people. Douglas fought to integrate restaurants in Washington, D.C., and she was the first white representative in the House to hire African Americans as staff members.

But once World War II was over, and the Communist "Red Scare" was sweeping the country, Douglas found her liberal beliefs under attack. Her opponents called her the "Pink Lady," implying she was a Communist sympathizer. In 1950, she ran for the open U.S. Senate seat in California against another representative, Republican Richard Nixon, who would one day become president of the United States. Nixon latched onto the Pink Lady nickname. In fact, he said she was "pink right down to her underwear." He did a good job of making the voters doubt Helen Douglas, and he won the election by more than 700,000 votes.

But she may have had the last laugh. During the campaign she tagged him "Tricky Dick," a name that haunted him throughout his career. When a political scandal called Watergate broke in 1973, during Nixon's second term as president, he became the first president to have to resign his office, and many people thought the nickname was well deserved.

African American citizens sitting in the rear of the bus, in compliance with Florida segregation law, ca. 1956.

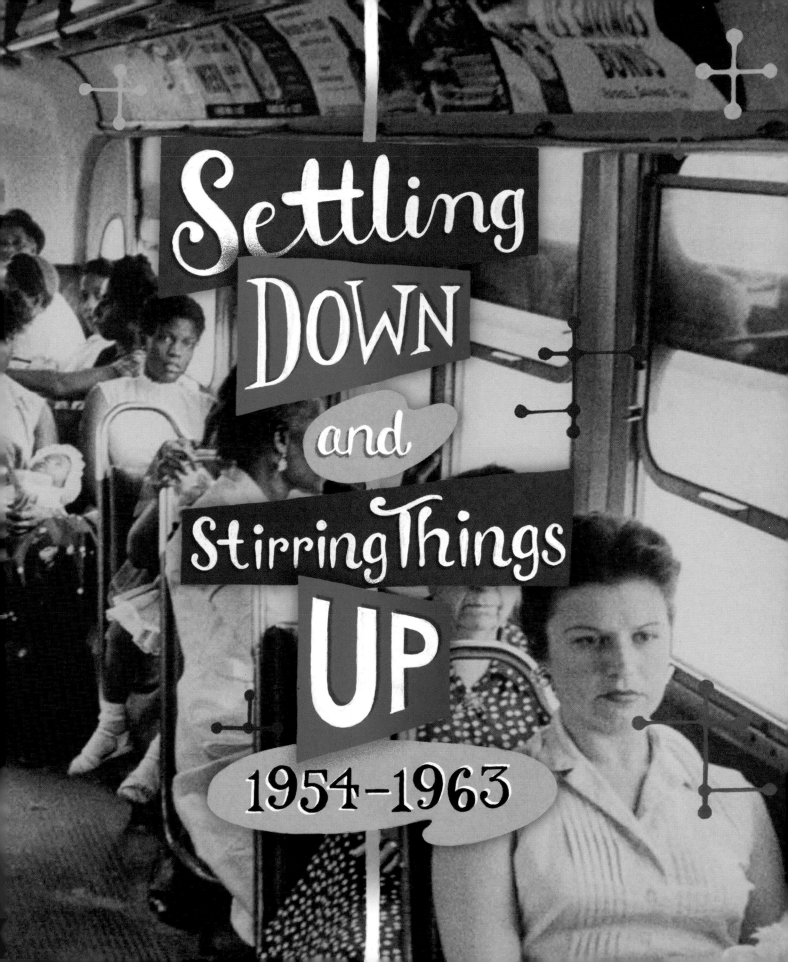

Settling Down and Stirring Things Up

1954–1963

As the decade of the 1950s moved into its middle years, there was a yearning, after the tough times of the Depression and World War II, to get back to "normal." For many people, that meant the husband at work and the wife at home with the children. There were too many returning servicemen who needed employment to let jobs be "wasted" on women.

One voice against that notion was New Jersey Representative Mary Norton. When the war was over, she said, "Women can't be Sitting-Room Sarahs or Kitchen Katies. They have homes to keep up . . . but they have their world to make." She warned that women being pushed "back into a corner" would be "heartbreaking."

Despite Norton's words, many women were happy to get back to taking care of their husbands and families. But some women liked the feeling of independence that working gave them and didn't want to return to the way things were.

Women who wanted to work outside the home had few role models. All they had to do in the 1950s was turn on that fabulous new invention, television, to see that they were supposed to be like Mrs. Anderson on *Father Knows Best* or Mrs. Cleaver on *Leave It to Beaver*: housewives.

So it's no surprise that during the 1950s and early 1960s, the number of women going to Washington hardly rose at all. And most of them still got there because their husbands died.

Until 1941, there were never more than ten women in Congress at the same time. Ten women to more than 500 men. How much progress had been made by the middle of the twentieth century? In 1955, seventeen women were sworn into Congress. One of those women was Martha Griffiths, a Democrat from Michigan. On the day of the swearing in, she sat next to one of the male representatives. He glumly said, "At this rate, it won't be any time before you ladies have the majority here."

Representative Griffiths couldn't believe her ears. The majority? Really? She asked the Library of Congress to figure out just how long it would take women to have the majority in Congress at the rate they were entering. The answer soon came back.

It would take 432 years!

But as the 1950s rolled into the 1960s, something was changing in the country. Things were beginning to shift. African Americans—the accepted term then was Negroes—were ready to do something about being America's second-class citizens. They had fought and died in war. They paid their taxes. Why did they have to live lives separate and not at all equal? Why did they face prejudice in all parts of the country every day?

African Americans had been fighting for their civil rights since the end of the Civil War. But moving forward was a long, slow process. In 1954, the Supreme Court of the United States handed down a ruling in *Brown v. Board of Education* that made separation of the races in public schools illegal across the country. That didn't stop school segregation, especially in the South. But by the late 1950s, protests over many forms of segregation began to take place.

A famous protest was started by a woman named Rosa Parks in Montgomery, Alabama. Rejecting the idea of having to move to the back of the bus so white passengers could sit down in the front, Rosa Parks let herself be arrested for refusing to give up her seat. That started a bus boycott that lasted for almost a year and led to the integration of the Montgomery bus system.

In 1960, four young black college students sat down at a whites-only lunch counter at a Woolworth's five-and-dime in Greensboro, North Carolina. They wanted some coffee. They didn't get it, but the students sat there. The next day they came back with thirty more students. Sixty-six showed up the next day. The store manager closed the store rather than serve the students.

But the protests went on. There were boycotts. Marches. Freedom Riders, black and white, got on buses to protest segregation, but the riders were beaten in Alabama. Still the protests grew, and under the leadership of Dr. Martin Luther King, Jr., the momentum for change reached critical mass. Dr. King gave his famous "I Have a Dream" speech on the National Mall on August 28, 1963—as he put it, "the greatest demonstration for freedom in the history of our nation." It seemed as if the wheels of racial progress had finally begun to roll.

Women, too, began to wonder about their role in society. Maybe, as many of the women who served in Congress had already shown, not all women were supposed to live the same kinds of lives.

Then, in the middle of all this upheaval, a shocking, horrible thing happened. President John F. Kennedy was assassinated in Dallas, Texas, on Friday, November 22, 1963. A stunned America watched events play out on their television sets. The assassination was something that would leave a deep emotional scar on the nation.

Members of Congress, men and women, were just as shocked as the rest of the country. The president's flag-covered mahogany casket was brought to the Capitol Building rotunda to lie in state on Sunday and Monday before the funeral. More than 250,000 people, many waiting in line for more than ten hours, passed by the casket to pay their respects.

Senator Margaret Chase Smith always wore a fresh red rose in her lapel. On Monday morning, before the funeral, she walked into the silent Senate chamber, removed the rose, and placed it on the desk where John Kennedy had sat when he'd served as the senator from Massachusetts.

CHAPTER 7 — CARRYING THE BANNER

FLORENCE DWYER
FRANCES PAYNE BOLTON
MARGUERITE CHURCH

When the Civil War ended in 1865, a handful of black men were elected to the U.S. Congress from the Southern states. But soon the white power structure regrouped. Through intimidation and restrictive laws, it became difficult for blacks to vote in the South and almost impossible for them to be elected to office.

By 1900, no African American men were left serving in the U.S. Congress. However, between 1929 and 1955 five African American men from Northern states were elected to the House of Representatives: three from Illinois, one from Michigan, and the most famous, from New York, Adam Clayton Powell, Jr., who stayed in the House for almost thirty years.

During the 1950s and 1960s, the civil rights movement gathered strength. Laws needed to be changed, and many white congressmen and -women took up the civil rights cause. Although Democrats are today traditionally associated with furthering the cause of civil rights, three congresswomen who carried the banner were Republicans. One was a representative from New Jersey, Florence Dwyer.

Flo, as she was known, got to the U.S. House of Representatives on her own steam. In fact, her opponent for the seat in the 1956 primary was another woman. Two women running for the same seat was still a rare occurrence.

Congresswoman Dwyer was a supporter of civil rights from the start of her first term. She introduced a bill that called for a commission to look into the problem of voting rights for African Americans in the South. She also spoke out against

FLORENCE DWYER

the poll tax. (Making people have to pay for voting was a way Southern local governments suppressed voting by poor blacks and whites.)

At a time when the U.S. government was frightened by the thought of Communism winning the Cold War, Flo Dwyer knew that it was important that America have its own house in order. "If freedom has any meaning at all, if our opposition to world communism is at all justifiable, then we have no alternative but to make secure for all Americans—regardless of race or color or religion or national origin or economic status—the practice and opportunity of full freedom."

And she thought that statement was just as true for women. She fought for equal pay and supported an Equal Rights Amendment to the Constitution that said there could be no discrimination because of a person's gender. But when it came to running for office—she ran for and won eight terms in the House—she didn't campaign as a woman. "I'm campaigning on my record," she said. "[I]f I can't take on any man running against me, I don't deserve to represent the women and men of the country."

* * * * * *

Frances Payne Bolton came to Congress from the Cleveland area of Ohio. Her husband, Chester Bolton, died in 1939, and she was appointed to her late husband's seat by Republican leaders because, as she said, "they were sure I'd get tired of politics . . . and flit on to something else."

Bolton did not flit. She won the election on her own in 1940, and she stayed in Congress for twenty-nine years.

Widely traveled and well-read, she was one of the richest women in the United States. Her range of interests went much further than that of most people of the time, men or women. She wanted to know about everything—from Buddhism in Asia to what life was like in Africa.

Her interest in health care led to the Bolton Act, which provided millions of dollars in funds to nursing schools all over the country. The act also created the U.S. Cadet Nurse Corps to train nurses to assist during World War II. Five years after the Bolton Act went into effect, more than 124,000 nurses had been trained. Representative Bolton made sure that African Americans had an equal chance to enter the corps.

During a visit to South Africa in 1955, Frances Bolton saw for herself the dehumanizing practice of apartheid, which separated that country's black and white citizens. And if segregation wasn't good for South Africa, it certainly wasn't good for her own country. She wanted America to be better than that.

She said in a speech before the United Nations, "Negro Americans in the U.S. are truly Americans who would not change their heritage if they could. We are learning that as we rub shoulders we can experience that which can be gained only when we come together. Prejudice must be put down wherever it raises its head."

With all her money, Frances Bolton could have lived a life of luxury. Instead, she opted for a life of service. She also made sure that part of her fortune provided scholarships for young people no matter their sex, race, or religion. As for her own religious beliefs, she summed them up like this, "[Y]ou and I are part and parcel of the stream of Universal Life—as water drops are part of the Great Sea."

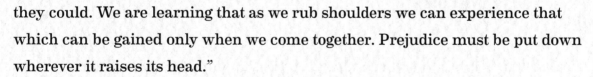

* * * * * *

When Senator Ralph Church died of a heart attack during a congressional committee meeting in 1950, Republicans in Illinois persuaded his wife, Marguerite, to run for his seat. Marguerite Church was clear-eyed about what she was getting into: "If a man had . . . made a mistake,

MARGUERITE CHURCH

you would have said he is stupid. If I make a mistake, you will say she is a woman."

Church, who had worked closely with her husband while he was in office, handily won the election for her husband's seat that same year. Once in Congress, her great interest was foreign affairs, and even though she was a Republican, she was a strong supporter of Democratic President Kennedy's brand-new program known as the Peace Corps, which sent college students to underdeveloped countries to help with educational and technological needs. Infuriated when a fellow representative ridiculed the not-yet-funded program by calling it "a Kiddie Corps," Church gave a rousing speech on the floor of the House to support it. She called the Peace Corps an example of Americanism that would show people in faraway lands what it meant to be free. Many House members who had been undecided voted for the Peace Corps bill after Representative Church made her speech.

But Marguerite Church didn't forget the young people at home. A supporter of civil rights, she made a small but important gesture in 1957 when she decided to ask six young African American newsboys who worked around Washington to lunch in the House dining room. The staff in the Capitol Building told her

there was no way her "guests" could be served. "Well," she replied, "I certainly do not intend to tell them that they can't luncheon in the dining room of their own Capitol."

And with that, she whisked the boys (among the first African Americans to be guests in the House dining room) to a table, and they all sat down and had lunch.

CHAPTER 8
MISSOURI AND MICHIGAN
LEONOR K. SULLIVAN
MARTHA WRIGHT GRIFFITHS

Two women came to the House of Representatives in the mid-1950s and stayed long enough to make their marks.

In 1952, Leonor Sullivan was the first woman to be elected to Congress from the "Show Me" state of Missouri. Her husband, John, had been a Democratic representative. She had been his aide and campaign manager. After he died in 1951, she tried to get his supporters to back her in a special election. But the political bosses weren't interested in supporting her. It wasn't personal: "We don't have anything against you," they told Sullivan, "we just want to win."

Well, the male candidate they chose didn't win. In the next election cycle, 1952, Leonor Sullivan beat out seven other Democrats in the primary. Then in the general election she beat the Republican candidate for her husband's old seat. She won the next eleven elections and stayed in the House until 1977.

When she was a girl, Leonor's family of nine children had to pinch pennies. When she got to Congress, Leonor Sullivan had one passion: she wanted to protect consumers, especially the poor. She wanted to make sure that the food and products people bought were safe, so in 1957 she helped write an amendment to the Food and Drug Act that required manufacturers to show that the ingredients in their products were safe. She also worked very hard to pass legislation that would begin a food stamp program. In 1959, that bill was passed. During the 1960s, she fought to make sure that banks were honest with their customers, and she was an early supporter of the right of women to earn the same pay for the same work as men.

LEONOR K. SULLIVAN

After twenty-four years in Congress, Leonor Sullivan decided not to run for office again. She said she was going to go home to St. Louis and live in her house that sat upon a bluff overlooking the Missouri River. And that's exactly what she did.

* * * * * * *

Martha Wright Griffiths (introduced earlier) showed what a woman could do when she got into a position of power. Young Martha lived on a Missouri farm until the house the Wrights were living in was struck by lightning. So her family moved to the "city," a town of about 1,500 people. Her parents were mail carriers, and they took in boarders to help pay Martha's tuition at the University of Missouri. It was important to her mother that Martha be able to make her own way in the world without being dependent on a man.

Both Martha and her husband, Hicks Griffiths, graduated from the University of Michigan law school, where Martha was the only woman in her class. She and Hicks both became lawyers in Detroit, and when she was asked why she wasn't a homemaker, she retorted, "I saw my mother work. I saw my grandmother work. I never thought about staying home and keeping house."

But both Martha and her husband were furious when they learned that even though they worked at the same law firm and did the same job, his salary was more than hers just because, as Hicks's boss told him, he was the man of the house.

Before she ran for a seat in the U.S. Congress, Martha Griffiths served as a representative to the Michigan legislature and as a judge. Then in 1954, she was elected to the U.S. House of Representatives and went to Washington to serve in Congress. Once there, she served on some of the most important committees in the House, especially the House Ways and Means Committee, helping to decide how to raise and spend the government's money. Being a member of the committee made her one of the most powerful women in Congress.

MARTHA WRIGHT GRIFFITHS

Griffiths was particularly interested in using her power to make laws that were more equitable for women. For instance, when she learned about how Social Security benefits were distributed, she was shocked. When a man died, his dependent children received benefits. But when a woman covered by Social Security died, her children received nothing. Griffiths worked hard to pass a law that made sure that this was changed.

She was also a champion of women in 1964. When the House Judiciary Committee began debating the Civil Rights Bill that would help stop racial discrimination, she made sure an amendment that would stop discrimination against women also be a part of the bill.

And in 1970, Martha Griffiths got the votes needed to bring the Equal Rights Amendment to a vote in the House of Representatives. The ERA, as it was called, said neither local, state, nor federal law could deny equal rights on account of sex. Getting the vote was the first step in making the ERA a part of the United States Constitution.

That never happened. But it wasn't Martha Griffiths's fault.

Banner on Fifth Avenue in New York City, commemorating the fiftieth anniversary of women's suffrage in the U.S., 1970.

ith the death of John F. Kennedy, Vice President Lyndon Johnson became president of the United States. It was no easy task to step into the shoes of the murdered young president. But Lyndon Johnson was a skillful politician who had spent many years in Congress. One thing he was very good at was turning bills into laws.

President Johnson set an ambitious legislative agenda. His successes changed the face of the United States forever. In 1964, Americans, black and white, wanted to see laws in place that would guarantee citizens their constitutional rights. When President Johnson took office, one of the first ways he found to honor President Kennedy was by calling for passage of the Civil Rights Bill, legislation begun by the late president. The bill passed the House of Representatives but stumbled in the Senate, where Southern senators wanted individual states to be allowed to make their own decisions on civil rights, not the federal government. Finally, a compromise was reached, and on July 2, 1964, the Civil Rights Act passed.

It was a groundbreaker!

No longer could public places refuse service to anyone because of race, color, or religion. That meant restaurants, shops, theaters, buses, and all government facilities had to treat everyone equally. By law, public schools and housing were open to everyone (though some people found ways around this). And when it came to jobs, employers could no longer discriminate by race, religion, or gender. (Thank Martha Griffiths for helping that last one get into the bill.)

In November 1964, Lyndon Johnson was elected in a landslide. He proposed what he called the "Great Society." The aims of the Great Society were big. Huge! President Johnson wanted to eliminate poverty and racial injustice in America.

The Civil Rights Act was part of the Great Society agenda. In 1965, Congress passed the Voting Rights Act, which made it easier for African Americans to vote. It outlawed the roadblocks, such as literacy tests and poll taxes, that some Southern states had put up to prevent people of color from exercising their voting rights.

President Johnson also proclaimed a War on Poverty. He wanted more opportunities for people to rise in society. Better health care and education were part of the fronts in that domestic war.

But the United States was already involved in another war, the Vietnam War. It started out small in the early 1960s and was supposed to prevent

Vietnam, a country in Southeast Asia, from becoming Communist. Under President Johnson the war got very big and very expensive. It was costing billions of dollars and thousands of lives.

Vietnam was an unpopular war. A growing number of

Americans didn't want their young men fighting in a war that didn't seem to have much point or an end in sight. President Johnson became unpopular, because of both the war and spending so much money on his programs at home.

The year 1968 was one of the most tumultuous years in U.S. history. President Johnson was planning to run for reelection, but by March he saw he had little chance of winning. He withdrew from the campaign. In April, America—and the larger world, too—was shattered by the assassination of Dr. Martin Luther King, Jr., in Memphis, Tennessee. Rioting broke out across the country.

Another horror came in June. President Kennedy's younger brother Robert, who was waging a strong run to be the Democrats' candidate for president, was assassinated in Los Angeles, California. By August, when the Democrats met in Chicago to nominate their candidate for president, the country was in turmoil. Protesters had come to Chicago, and they were met by the local police with violent force.

The Democratic candidate, Vice President Hubert Humphrey, lost in November to Republican Richard Nixon. Nixon said he would end the war in Vietnam, but the war went on and even expanded. Still, Nixon won a second term in 1972.

Then, in 1974, as result of a political scandal known as Watergate, Richard Nixon became the first president in American history to resign his office.

As the unrest of the 1960s rolled into the 1970s, one of the biggest movements of the decade picked up steam. The women's movement encouraged women to think about their place in society, insisted on equal pay for equal work, and demanded more opportunities for women in schools and in the workplace.

The women's movement brought more women into Congress, and these women were in many ways different from the ones who had come before: they were better educated, they had more experience running for office, and for the first time, women of color joined their ranks.

The numbers of women in Congress were still small. But change was in the air.

CHAPTER 9 · A DIFFERENT KIND OF PIONEER

PATSY TAKEMOTO MINK

Black men had served in the U.S. Congress. White women had served. And, of course, white men had held the vast majority of seats since the first Congress convened in 1789.

Then, in 1965, Democratic Representative Patsy Mink arrived in Washington, D.C. She came from Hawaii (which had been a state only since 1959). Of Japanese descent, she was the first woman of color and the first Asian American woman to be elected to the House of Representatives.

Patsy had always been a fighter. When she went to college at the University of Nebraska right after World War II, she learned she was going to have to live in segregated housing because she wasn't white. That made Patsy mad. She wrote letters to the local newspapers and the school authorities. She made speeches. As she herself said, she was somebody who was going to "stir up trouble" if she saw injustice. Soon she had many others in the university community behind her, and while she was still at school, the housing policy was reversed.

A lawyer who had served in Hawaii's State Senate, Mink first ran for Congress in 1964. Some of the women in Congress had gotten their political feet wet by being their husbands' campaign managers. In a refreshing turn of events, Patsy's husband, John Mink, was her campaign manager.

Patsy Mink won her congressional election and went on to serve twelve years in the House in her first

PATSY TAKEMOTO MINK

go-around. In 1976, she tried for a Senate seat but didn't win. So she stayed in Hawaii for almost twenty years, keeping active in local politics. Then, in 1990, Mink was reelected to the House, where she served until her death in 2002.

Patsy Mink was a proud liberal. During her first stay in the House, she supported the programs of Lyndon Johnson's Great Society, but she was a vocal critic of the war in Vietnam. Her big focus was making sure that laws were passed that gave women equality in educational opportunities, including athletics. A 1972 law was renamed the Patsy T. Mink Equal Opportunity in Education Act in 2002, to honor all that Mink had done to make sure there would be no discrimination in any school program funded by the federal government.

One of the most visible results of this act is that women's sports teams in schools now receive funding in ways that equal that of men's teams.

When she first came to the House, Patsy Mink was one of only eight women serving in Congress. That made her feel she had "a special burden" to speak for all women. "I always felt that we were serving a dual role in Congress, representing our own districts and, at the same time, having to voice the concerns of the total population of women in the country."

Her legacy to the young women of America who participate in sports programs continues to this day.

CHAPTER 10

"UNBOUGHT AND UNBOSSED"

SHIRLEY CHISHOLM

When a college professor asked Shirley St. Hill if she had ever thought about going into politics, she replied, "You forget two things. I'm black and I'm a woman."

Shirley might have added a few more things. The Brooklyn-born teacher had an accent, having been raised on the Caribbean island of Barbados, and there were few political role models for her to follow—and none of them were black women.

Still, Shirley, later to marry Conrad Chisholm, was interested in politics and she became a member of local New York political clubs, in time winning a seat in the New York legislature. But Shirley thought she'd be more effective on the national stage. So in 1968, when a new congressional district in New York was created, Shirley decided to run for the seat. The people who lived in this district were African American, Jewish, and Latino. She thought the voters would like the fact that she was independent and didn't owe any of the party bosses anything. Her campaign slogan was "Shirley Chisholm: Unbought and Unbossed."

After a hard fight in both the primary and general elections, Shirley won. She would be the first black woman to walk the hallowed halls of the United States Congress as a representative!

As soon as she got to Congress, Shirley Chisholm did something radical. She staffed her office from top to bottom with women. No other member of Congress in the

SHIRLEY CHISHOLM

history of the House had done that. Most hadn't hired any women at all, except for secretaries. But Representative Chisholm's decision to hire only women, both black and white, showed that you didn't need a man to get things done in the House.

Shirley Chisholm had come to Congress to stir things up, and during her time, she kept on stirring. By the late 1960s, approximately 3 million servicepeople were fighting in Vietnam, some enlisting but most being drafted into the army. Chisholm thought the war, as she put it in her first speech to Congress in 1969, was "immoral, unjust, and unnecessary." She also resented the fact that the war's high price tag took much-needed money from housing and food programs and Head Start, which helped poor children get a jump on education.

In 1972, Shirley Chisholm made a revolutionary decision. She decided to run for president. Oh, she knew she couldn't win. But she felt strongly that the political landscape in America needed change and color. She wanted to speak up for the poor, the minorities, and those against the Vietnam War. Even though losing was never in doubt, she campaigned hard, and at the Democratic convention, she picked up 152 delegate votes—a small percentage of the more than 3,000 votes needed to win the nomination, but symbolic nevertheless.

Shirley Chisholm stayed in Congress until 1982. In a 2004 documentary, she said: "When I die, I want to be remembered as a woman who lived in the twentieth century and who dared to be a catalyst for change. I don't want to be remembered as the first black woman who went to Congress, and I don't even want to be remembered as the first woman who happened to be black to make a bid for the presidency. I want to be remembered as a woman who fought for change in the twentieth century. That's what I want."

You got it, Shirley!

CHAPTER 11 — JOINING SHIRLEY

BARBARA JORDAN
YVONNE BRATHWAITE BURKE
CARDISS COLLINS

hree more African American women followed Shirley Chisholm into the House of Representatives. Texan Barbara Jordan arrived in 1972, the first black woman elected to Congress from a Southern state. She was a powerful orator who had honed her skills in church and in school, taking part in public-speaking contests. It was her impressive voice that first introduced the freshman House member to the rest of the country.

It happened during the impeachment trial of President Richard Nixon, which began on July 25, 1974. Television sets all over the country were turned on; people wanted to watch the opening statements of

BARBARA JORDAN

the House Judiciary Committee, which would decide whether to bring Articles of Impeachment against President Nixon for crimes he had committed during the political scandal Watergate.

Watergate was the name of the building complex that housed the offices of the Democratic National Committee. During the 1972 presidential campaign, several men, directed by the Republican president's campaign staff, broke into the office in an effort to learn about the Democrats' financing and strategies. An attempted cover-up led to more scandal, including the discovery of White House tape recordings that seemed to prove President Nixon had been aware of illegal activities. If the president was impeached (that is, charged with a crime) by the House of Representatives, he would then have a trial in the Senate, which would have the final decision on whether he would be removed from office.

Sitting on the House Judiciary Committee, which would decide Nixon's fate, was Barbara Jordan. The Judiciary Committee was a plum assignment, not usually given to freshman representatives. But former president Lyndon Johnson had seen potential in Jordan and called in a favor to have her appointed to the committee.

Representative Jordan began her statement with the eyes of the country on her. The first thing she noted was how far the country had come during its almost-200-year history, demonstrated by the fact she was sitting where she was: "Earlier today, we heard the beginning of the Preamble to the Constitution of the United States: 'We, the People.' It's a very eloquent beginning. But when that document was completed on the seventeenth of September in 1787, I was not included in that 'We, the people.' I felt somehow for many years that George Washington and Alexander Hamilton just left me out by mistake. But through the process of amendment, interpretation, and court decision, I have finally been included in 'We, the people.'"

After discussing the nature and history of impeachment, and going over the facts of Watergate, Jordan went on to ask, "Has the president committed offenses, and planned, and directed, and acquiesced in a course of conduct which the Constitution will not tolerate? . . . We should now forthwith proceed to answer the question. It is reason, and not passion, which must guide our deliberations, guide our debate, and guide our decision."

As evidence mounted against him, President Nixon decided not to wait to be impeached. He resigned instead.

At the 1976 Democratic convention, Barbara Jordan gave a

IT IS REASON, AND NOT PASSION, WHICH MUST GUIDE OUR DELIBERATIONS.

speech so stirring, it is considered one of the best in U.S. political history. In it, she made a plea for all citizens, no matter their race, sex, or religion, to come together to form what she called a national community: "In this election year, we must define the 'common good' and begin again to shape a common future. Let each person do his or her part. If one citizen is unwilling to participate, all of us are going to suffer. For the American idea, though it is shared by all of us, is realized in each one of us."

Barbara Jordan was diagnosed with multiple sclerosis in 1973 and left the House in 1979 to return to Texas. Despite her illness, she continued working, as a professor at the University of Texas and as chair of the U.S. Commission on Immigration Reform in 1994. She received many honors before her death in 1996, but perhaps the greatest is that her words live on.

* * * * * * *

Yvonne Brathwaite Burke, a Democrat who was elected to the House of Representatives in 1972, had several firsts during her time there. She was the first African American woman to be elected to national office from the state of California. She was also the first woman to have a baby while serving in Congress. After Autumn Burke was born, her mother became the first woman in Congress to be granted maternity leave.

Being a mother didn't stop Congresswoman Burke from taking on a full share of responsibility. She was elected chair of the Congressional Black Caucus, a group of representatives whose goal is to positively influence events and legislation important to African Americans. She worked hard for laws that would help women, the poor, and minorities. Her most important piece of legislation was to make sure that women and other minorities had a chance to bid on government construction contracts, contracts

YVONNE BRATHWAITE BURKE

worth a lot of money that were usually issued only to companies owned by white men.

In 1978, when Autumn Burke was four years old, Congresswoman Burke decided that traveling back and forth between Washington, D.C., and California made it difficult to raise a child. She decided not to run for reelection. This didn't end her political career though. Back in California, she served on the Los Angeles Board of Supervisors, their city council.

Yvonne Burke could sum up her philosophy in a few sentences: "When I walk into a room, I assume I have to prove myself. I know that. I'm accustomed to that. But I also know I can prove myself."

* * * * * *

Many people remember Shirley Chisholm, Barbara Jordan, and Yvonne Burke.

But even while she was serving a record-breaking twelve terms in Congress, beginning with her appointment in 1973 after her husband's death, Cardiss Collins remained relatively unknown. She was the sort of legislator who didn't seek the limelight.

Democrat Cardiss Collins was the first African American woman sent to the House from Illinois. She did her job quietly and consistently, making sure she spent plenty of time talking to the people she represented back home in her district on Chicago's West Side. She fought for antipoverty programs, universal health coverage, and women's issues. Collins also wanted young women to have the same rights as young men when it came to college sports, and she introduced bills to make sure that happened. In 1994, when Collins's career in Congress was nearing its end, she was inducted into the Women's Sports Hall of Fame for her hard work in this area.

CARDISS COLLINS

Two of the women who came to Congress in the 1970s made such an impression, they were remembered long after their terms of service were over.

Brash and noted for wearing big hats, Democrat Bella Abzug blew into the House of Representatives after winning the 1970 election in her New York City district. She knew just what she wanted to accomplish. Bella was "pro": pro–women's rights, gay rights, reproductive rights, and civil rights. Before coming to Congress, she had worked as a lawyer in New York, taking cases, sometimes without payment, to represent the poor and the disenfranchised.

There was one thing she was "anti," and that was war.

THIS WOMAN'S PLACE IS IN THE HOUSE— THE HOUSE OF REPRESENTATIVES!

Her campaign slogan was "This woman's place is in the House—the House of Representatives!" On her first day in the House, in 1971, she introduced legislation that demanded an end to the Vietnam War.

Bella Abzug also was unafraid of taking on powerful men. J. Edgar Hoover, the long-time head of the F.B.I., was feared by many in the country, who knew that he was not above using the Bureau to settle personal scores. That didn't stop Abzug from asking for an investigation into whether he was still able to do his job. And when the Watergate scandal broke, she was one of the first to call for the impeachment of President Richard Nixon.

After three terms working tirelessly in the House, making friends and plenty of enemies, Bella Abzug decided in 1977 to run for the U.S. Senate from the state of New York. She lost, but she spent the next twenty years of her life organizing for the causes she believed in, particularly the women's movement.

Bella Abzug had a clear idea of what people thought of her: "There are those who say I'm impatient, impetuous, uppity, rude, profane, brash, and overbearing. Whether I'm any of these things, or all of them, you can decide for yourself. But whatever I am—and this ought to be made very clear—I am a very serious woman."

BELLA ABZUG

* * * * * *

If there was one woman in Congress who was the opposite of Bella Abzug, at least outwardly, it was Republican Millicent Fenwick from New Jersey. Where Abzug was the daughter of Jewish parents who had immigrated to the United States from Russia, Fenwick's family had a long, distinguished history in the United States, going back to Colonial times. Abzug's personal style was flamboyant, while the elegant Fenwick worked first as a high-fashion model and then as an editor at *Vogue* magazine. In 1948, she wrote a book on proper etiquette.

But when it came to their causes, Democrat Bella and liberal Republican Millicent shared similar sensibilities, and they became friends. Both worked hard for civil rights, women's rights, and human rights. One of Congresswoman Fenwick's most important areas of concentration during her four terms in the House was her work on human rights abuses behind the Iron Curtain, the term used to describe the barrier the Soviet Union put between countries it controlled in Eastern Europe and capitalist countries in the West. Her congressional bill that created a commission to monitor human rights violations, was, she said, her proudest achievement.

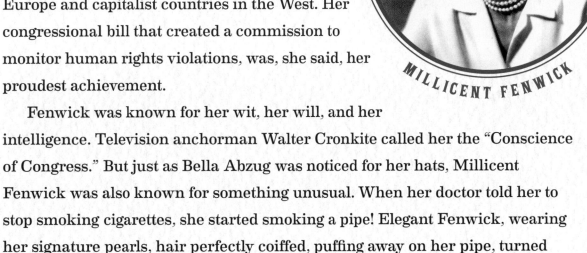

MILLICENT FENWICK

Fenwick was known for her wit, her will, and her intelligence. Television anchorman Walter Cronkite called her the "Conscience of Congress." But just as Bella Abzug was noticed for her hats, Millicent Fenwick was also known for something unusual. When her doctor told her to stop smoking cigarettes, she started smoking a pipe! Elegant Fenwick, wearing her signature pearls, hair perfectly coiffed, puffing away on her pipe, turned heads all over Washington, D.C.

CHAPTER 13
A WOMAN OF HER TIME
PATRICIA SCHROEDER

During the 1970s, thanks to the women's movement, barriers were breaking down in all fields: employment, education, sports, politics. But that didn't mean women were welcome in traditionally male-populated environments.

In 1976, three years after she had come to the House of Representatives as a Democrat from Colorado, Patricia Schroeder and her husband were given tickets to the awards dinner at the Touchdown Club, frequented by many members of Congress. But the Touchdown Club and its dinner were for men only. When she tried to enter the dinner, Representative Pat Schroeder was unceremoniously turned away.

She didn't like it, but Schroeder, familiar with the discrimination common in Congress—which she described as an "over-aged frat house"—was used to being insulted. One of the youngest representatives ever elected (she was only thirty-one years old), she was mocked as the first woman to wear pants instead of a skirt or dress to the floor of the House, and as the mother of two young sons, she was criticized by some people for having a political career instead of being a stay-at-home mom.

In past decades, women in Congress might not always have been welcomed by their male counterparts, but were mostly treated politely. Now that women throughout American society were demanding their rights instead of asking for them, many men were getting hostile. This was true in Congress as well. When Pat Schroeder was

PATRICIA SCHROEDER

appointed to the Armed Services Committee,
the chairman, Edward Hébert from Louisiana,
actually made her and Ron Dellums, an African
American representative from California, share
one chair during the first meeting, because, he
said, "women and blacks were worth only half of
one regular Member" and deserved only half a
seat!

As Schroeder wrote later, "Nobody
else objected, and nobody offered to
scrounge up another chair."

Later, when she asked Chairman
Hébert if she could represent
the United States at an arms
treaty conference, he told her
he wouldn't let her represent the committee at a dogfight. Schroeder bided
her time, and several years later, with the help of like-minded congressional
colleagues, men and women, who had recently joined the committee, they
ousted Representative Hébert from his chairmanship.

During her time in Congress, Pat Schroeder tried to streamline the budget
of the Defense Department and fought against sexual harassment in the
armed services. But her major area of focus was helping women and families.
Knowing from personal experience how difficult it was to juggle a job and
family life, Schroeder worked long and hard to pass the Family and Medical
Leave Act, which allowed for up to eighteen weeks of unpaid leave to take care
of a newborn, a sick child, an aged parent, or other sick family member. For
the first time, women and men wouldn't have to worry about losing their jobs if
someone in their family needed their care.

By 1980, the country, with Republican Ronald Reagan as president, was
becoming more conservative, and Schroeder had to fight harder than ever to

move her bills forward. Still, she stayed in Congress, pushing for legislation she thought was important, before deciding in 1996 to move on.

But before she left the House, there was one honor she was anxious to receive.

Twenty years after she had been thrown out of the Touchdown Club award dinner, she became the first woman to receive the club's award for government service. It was presented (on bended knee) by the very man who had ordered her out!

"He told me how the club was hammered with letters from mothers, sisters and daughters after that night," Schroeder said. "He was a very good sport about the whole thing."

CHAPTER 14 — A POSSIBLE VICE PRESIDENT

GERALDINE FERRARO

eraldine Ferraro was elected to the House of Representatives in 1978. By 1984, she was the vice presidential nominee on the Democratic ticket headed by Walter Mondale. She was the first woman to run for vice president from one of the two major parties.

How did Geraldine Ferraro get so far so fast? She came to Congress from a middle-class, ethnically diverse section of Queens, New York. Most of the people who lived there leaned conservative. But her campaign slogan, "Finally, a tough Democrat," was a winner. Voters were impressed by the job Ferraro had done as a district attorney in the Special Victims Bureau, where she dealt with abuse against women and children.

Once she had taken her seat in Congress, Ferraro continued to fight hard for women, with a special focus on the elderly and children, and mocked the Republicans whose policies, she thought, were tilted against working women.

Her fellow members of the Democratic Party began to take notice of Geraldine Ferraro. They thought she was a straight shooter. She began to rise to prominence both in the party and in Congress, where she sat on the important Budget Committee.

As the 1984 presidential campaign got under way, many Democratic women in the country wanted to see a female on the national ticket. When Walter Mondale got the nomination, he had a list of several women who he thought might make good vice presidential candidates, including Patricia Schroeder. But he chose Geraldine Ferraro, in

GERALDINE FERRARO

part because he felt she would appeal not only to women but also to Italian Americans. Many people—including other women in Congress—thought Representative Ferraro didn't have enough experience for the second highest office in the land, especially in foreign affairs. When allegations of financial wrongdoing were made against her husband, the Democratic ticket went down in the polls. Mondale and Ferraro were beaten handily by President Ronald Reagan and Vice President George Bush, running for their second term.

After the election, Geraldine Ferraro left Congress, but she kept working, first as a lawyer, then as a television analyst, and, later, when called upon by President Bill Clinton in the 1990s, as a delegate to important global conferences.

PACIFIC STATE SENATOR,
PRAIRIE STATE SENATOR

MAURINE NEUBERGER
NANCY LANDON KASSEBAUM

In 1978, the more elite side of the Congress, the Senate, was—as usual—empty of women.

Hattie Caraway had lost her bid for reelection after a twelve-year run as a senator from Arkansas. Margaret Chase Smith had left the Senate in 1973. Several other women had come and gone after either filling out their husbands' terms or completing a term won in a special election. The only woman who came and stayed awhile was Democrat Maurine Neuberger from Oregon, who also won a special election in 1960 to finish her late husband's term but went on to win her own term and remained in the Senate until 1967, focusing on consumer issues, including sponsoring a bill that would put warning labels on cigarettes.

MAURINE NEUBERGER

NANCY LANDON KASSEBAUM

Then, in 1978, Nancy Landon Kassebaum came to the Senate and stayed for the next two decades.

Young Nancy Landon had grown up in Topeka, Kansas, in a home where politics was served up as regularly as breakfast, lunch, and dinner. Her father, Alf, was twice elected as the governor of the state and had run as the Republican candidate for president against Franklin Roosevelt in 1936.

When she married in 1956, Nancy lived on a

farm with her husband. She got some public service experience by serving on a local school board. After her divorce in the 1970s, she moved to D.C., working in the Senate office of Kansas Republican James Pearson.

In 1978, Senator Pearson retired, and Nancy Landon Kassebaum decided she wanted to go after that Senate seat. People said she'd never make it. Her experience was minimal, and she had eight Republican primary challengers for the nomination (including another woman) who all wanted the job as much as she did.

But Nancy had something the others did not: the well-respected political name of Landon. Nancy beat them all. The name was magic in the general election against her Democratic contender as well. Nancy knew it and acknowledged it. Her campaign slogan was: "A Fresh Face: A Trusted Kansas Name."

Despite the help her name gave her, Kassebaum could still claim bragging rights on being the first woman elected to a full term in the Senate who got there without first having a husband who had served in Congress.

Nancy Kassebaum was a Republican from a conservative state, but she was also her own person. She was pro-choice and believed a pregnant woman should have the right to decide whether she would or would not have the baby. She didn't mind working with Democrats such as Senator Ted Kennedy of Massachusetts on issues she believed in, like affordable health care.

Early in her career, she was appointed to one of most powerful and important Senate committees, Foreign Relations. Senator Kassebaum headed the Subcommittee on African Affairs. She didn't know much about Africa, but she soon learned. To help put an end to South Africa's practice of segregation called apartheid, she pushed the United States to impose economic sanctions or penalties on that country, putting pressure on the South African government to end the discrimination.

Nancy Kassebaum stayed in the Senate from 1978 to 1997. For much of that time, she was either the only woman or one of a few out of that one-hundred-person body. But she said she didn't think of herself as a woman senator. She was the United States senator from Kansas who happened to be a woman.

Sandra Day O'Connor, the first woman to serve on the Supreme Court, with the eight other justices, 1983.

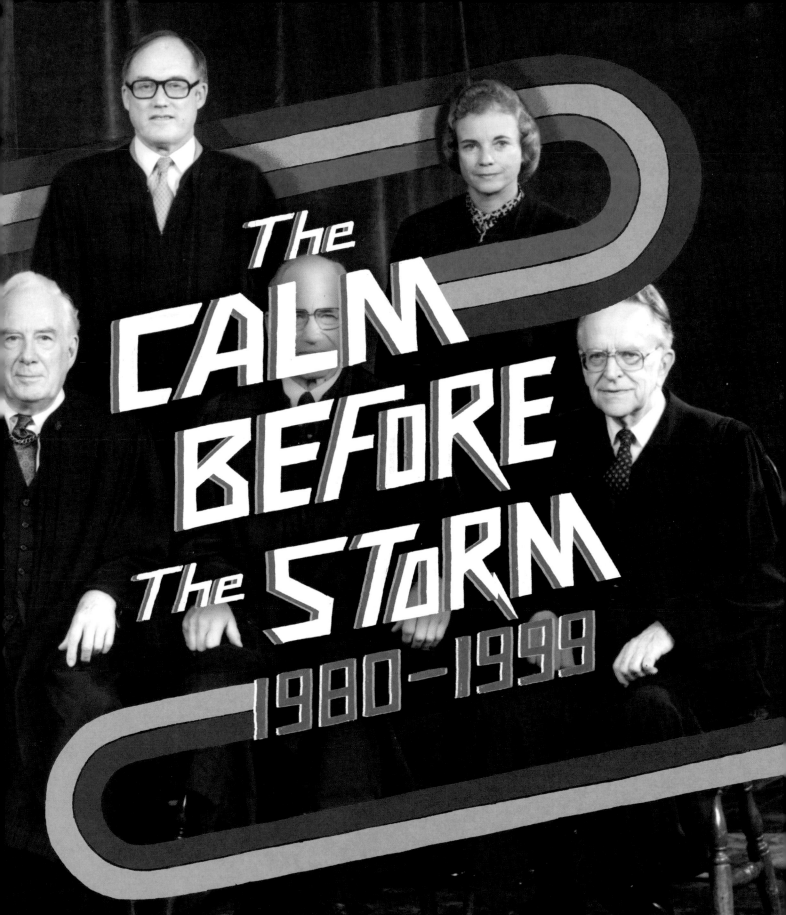

The CALM BEFORE The STORM 1980-1999

Throughout its history, the United States has faced wars, civil strife, economic ups and downs, and political scandals. The years from 1980 to 1999 were no different, but as we look back at the decades before the terrorist attack on September 11, 2001, they seem quiet in comparison to the events at the beginning of the twenty-first century. During this time, the country had three very different kinds of presidents.

Ronald Reagan, a former governor of California and a one-time actor, was elected president in 1980. A conservative Republican, Reagan spent much of his time on foreign affairs. He famously called the Soviet Union "an evil empire," because it imposed its power beyond its borders. President Reagan supported anti-Communist revolutions around the globe.

In 1987, one of the most dramatic moments of the Cold War occurred. Standing near Germany's Berlin Wall, which divided democratic West Berlin from Communist East Berlin, President Reagan challenged the Soviet Union leader, Mikhail Gorbachev: "Tear down this wall!"

By 1989, the Soviet Union was on the verge of collapse. In Germany, the Berlin Wall, one of the great symbols of the Cold War, indeed began to be dismantled.

At home, President Reagan believed in cutting taxes and spending less on government programs. He did not support the Equal Rights Amendment, which was passed in Congress in 1972 and was waiting to be ratified by the states. He did take one strong stand for women: he appointed the first woman to the Supreme Court.

Along with the president and Congress, the third and equal branch of the United States government is the Supreme Court. Eight justices and one Chief Justice make up the Court, which helps decide the laws of the land. The Supreme Court first began its work in 1789. For almost two hundred years after that, the only judges who sat on the Supreme Court were men. Then, in 1981, President Reagan appointed Sandra Day O'Connor to the court. When she graduated from Stanford Law School in

1952, O'Connor had had trouble finding a job as a lawyer because she was a woman. By the time of her appointment to the Supreme Court, however, the country was ready to see a woman in one of the nation's most important jobs.

Ronald Reagan served as president for two terms. In 1988, his vice president, George Herbert Walker Bush, won the presidency. During his term in office, the Middle Eastern country of Iraq invaded its neighbor Kuwait. President Bush began rallying other countries to join him to fight Iraq. The Persian Gulf War was a short war in the first months of 1991 and succeeded in pushing Iraq out of Kuwait.

In 1992, Bill Clinton, the Democratic governor of Arkansas, beat George H. W. Bush (and a third-party candidate, businessman Ross Perot) for the presidency. President Clinton served two terms in office. He fought with Congress over spending, and for a short time the government was shut down. Although there was mostly peace and prosperity during President Clinton's eight years, he managed to divide the American people in 1998 when it was discovered he had had an intimate relationship with a young White House intern.

Republicans, who were the majority in the House of Representatives, felt this misstep was enough to impeach Mr. Clinton. But while the House can call for impeachment, it is the Senate that has to vote yes or no. In February 1999, the Senate, controlled by the Democrats, voted to let the president continue his term.

During the 1980s and 1990s, the United States was changing in exciting new ways. It was less segregated, with people's heritages more often celebrated than looked down upon. And a new innovation, the home computer, was changing the way people worked and played.

How were women doing? They were becoming a more visible force throughout American society. More college graduates. More doctors and lawyers. More women in business and in the media. That visibility was true in Congress as well. So many women were elected to the U.S. Congress in 1992, it became known as "the Year of the Woman."

16 THE YEAR OF THE WOMAN

CAROL MOSELEY BRAUN
DIANNE FEINSTEIN * BARBARA BOXER
PATTY MURRAY * BARBARA MIKULSKI
ILEANA ROS-LEHTINEN

In 1991, the U.S. Senate had two woman senators, Republican Nancy Kassebaum of Kansas and Democrat Barbara Mikulski of Maryland. Mikulski, the daughter of Polish-American immigrants, came to the Senate after first serving on the Baltimore City Council and, later, as a representative to the U.S. Congress from Maryland.

Then, in 1992, something happened that had never happened before. Four women won their Senate races! They would join Senators Kassebaum and Mikulski, bringing the total of women in the Senate to six, the highest number ever serving at one time. More astonishingly, one of the new senators was an African American and two came from the same state—California. Yes, both of California's senators were women!

When Carol Moseley Braun arrived in the Senate, there had been only one other African American senator during all of the twentieth century, Edward Brooke of Massachusetts. Senator Moseley Braun, a Democrat from Illinois, knew that just being elected as the first African American female senator made her a symbol of what was possible in America. She spent only one term in Congress, but Senator Moseley Braun used her time to work on civil rights issues and focus on legislation that would help families.

CAROL MOSELEY BRAUN

* * * * * * *

It's highly unusual that two senators from the same state would be running for seats during the same election, because the Constitution staggers senate

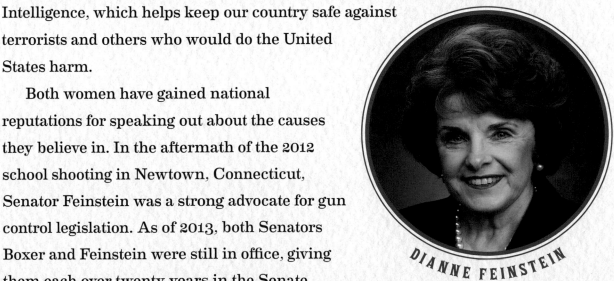

BARBARA BOXER

races so that states will always have one experienced senator in office. But Dianne Feinstein of California was running to fill out the term of Senator Pete Wilson, who had resigned to become the state's governor. Barbara Boxer was running for a full six-year term. On November 3, 1992, both women, both Democrats, won their elections.

Barbara Boxer came to the Senate from Northern California's Marin County, where she served as the district's representative to the U.S. House. Senator Boxer's focus in the Senate has been on issues affecting families, children, consumers, and the environment. She has the distinction of having won her 2004 election by the highest margin ever in a Senate race—6.9 million votes. Senator Boxer, who was once a journalist, has also published two novels—about politics, of course.

Dianne Feinstein ran for senator after serving as the mayor of San Francisco. She has sat on some of the Senate's most important committees, including the Appropriations Committee, which helps decide how the U.S. government will spend taxpayers' money, and the Select Committee on Intelligence, which helps keep our country safe against terrorists and others who would do the United States harm.

Both women have gained national reputations for speaking out about the causes they believe in. In the aftermath of the 2012 school shooting in Newtown, Connecticut, Senator Feinstein was a strong advocate for gun control legislation. As of 2013, both Senators Boxer and Feinstein were still in office, giving them each over twenty years in the Senate.

DIANNE FEINSTEIN

* * * * * * *

A mom in tennis shoes." That's what Patty Murray, an environmental and educational activist, was called by a local politician who scoffed at her for wanting to make a difference in their home state of Washington. Murray took those words as a challenge. In fact, "A Mom in Tennis Shoes" was her campaign slogan in her 1992 senatorial campaign. People liked the idea of a regular woman representing them. They liked it so much, in fact, that they elected her for three more six-year terms. The daughter of a disabled World War II vet, Murray has championed the cause of veterans' rights. She's also an advocate for better health care for all citizens.

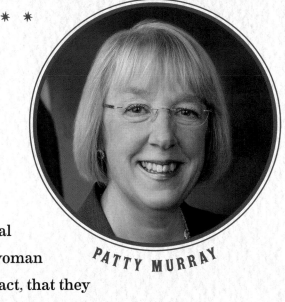

PATTY MURRAY

Along with the election of the six woman senators, the Year of the Woman took on more heft in the House of Representatives. Twenty-seven women were elected to the House, twenty-four of them for the first time!

With more experience in government than many of their predecessors, the new woman representatives were mostly Democrats who were swept into office with the new Democratic president, Bill Clinton. They were joining women like Republican Ileana Ros-Lehtinen, the first Hispanic American woman to serve in Congress, who came to the House of Representatives in 1989.

Vote Patty Murray "a MOM in TENNIS SHOES"

Welcome to LITTLE HAVANA U.S.A

* * * * * *

Ileana Ros-Lehtinen and her family had escaped Communist Cuba and its dictator, Fidel Castro, in 1960, when she was eight. Cuba has continued to be of great interest to her during her congressional career, and she supported measures that isolate Cuba until there is a change in its leadership. She has said, "I am a fierce opponent of the Castro regime . . . and other dictatorial regimes in Latin America that subvert the will of the people and seek to erode democratic institutions."

Even though newspaper headline writers liked the catchy phrase "Year of the Woman," not all the members of Congress appreciated that designation. Senator Barbara Mikulski of Maryland in particular wasn't pleased. "Calling 1992 the Year of the Woman makes it sound like the Year of the Caribou or the Year of the Asparagus," she commented tartly. "We're not a fad, a fancy, or a year."

ILEANA ROS-LEHTINEN

BARBARA MIKULSKI

And she was right. In the following decades, the number of women in Congress has continued to creep up. And Barbara Mikulski, twenty years after that statement was made, went on to become the longest-serving female in the U.S. Congress.

CHAPTER 17

MAINE—TWO WOMAN SENATORS

OLYMPIA SNOWE
SUSAN COLLINS

As in California on the West Coast, in the 1990s a new milestone was set on the East Coast. Maine had two women serving as senators. Olympia Snowe came first, elected in 1994. Susan Collins joined her in 1997.

Both women had interesting backgrounds.

* * * * * *

Snowe's childhood was a sad one. Her mother died of breast cancer when she was nine, and her father died a year later. Young Olympia was taken in by an uncle, who also died before she was grown.

Tragedy did not stop stalking her as an adult, either. Her husband, Peter Snowe, was a Republican legislator in the state of Maine. After just a few years of marriage, he was killed in an automobile accident. She ran for his seat and, at age twenty-six, found herself in the Maine House of Representatives. After a stint in the Maine Senate, in 1978 Snowe won a seat in the U.S. House. In Washington, D.C., she met her second husband, John McKernan, who would later become Maine's governor. From 1989 to 1995, Olympia Snowe had to juggle two very big jobs. She was both the first lady of Maine and a U.S. House representative.

In 1994, Representative Snowe became Senator Snowe after winning her first Senate election by a huge margin. In 2006, *Time* magazine named Olympia Snowe one of "America's

OLYMPIA SNOWE

10 Best Senators." She had a lot of firsts in her career, including first woman to serve in both houses of Maine's legislature as well as serving her state in both houses of the U.S. Congress and the first woman of Greek heritage to be elected to Congress. And she never lost an election during her thirty-four years in government.

* * * * * *

Susan Collins came from a political family. Growing up in Caribou, Maine, she saw her parents each serve as mayor of their town. Her dad was also a Maine legislator.

When she was a senior in high school, Collins participated in a program that changed her life: the United States Senate Youth Program. Each year, two student leaders are chosen to represent their states in Washington, D.C., and experience how government really works.

As Collins remembers the experience: "One of the highlights . . . is always the opportunity to meet with Senators from one's home

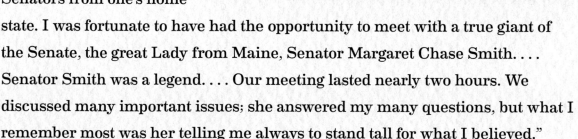

state. I was fortunate to have had the opportunity to meet with a true giant of the Senate, the great Lady from Maine, Senator Margaret Chase Smith. . . . Senator Smith was a legend. . . . Our meeting lasted nearly two hours. We discussed many important issues; she answered my many questions, but what I remember most was her telling me always to stand tall for what I believed."

Little did the teenage Susan Collins know that one day she would sit in the very Senate seat once held by Margaret Chase Smith.

During the 2000s, Snowe and Collins became two of the most influential senators in Washington, D.C. That's because as the Republican Party grew more and more conservative, the women were a rare species: moderate Republicans. Sometimes one or both of them voted with the Democrats, especially on social issues. Since they were swing voters (their vote could make the difference in whether a bill passed or not), their support on an issue was considered particularly valuable.

SUSAN COLLINS

Senators Snowe and Collins made their voices heard.

Democratic presidential hopefuls Senator Hillary Rodham Clinton and Senator Barack Obama before the start of their debate at the National Constitution Center in Philadelphia, 2008.

AN
UNSETTLING
Decade
2000–2010

everal events occurred in the years between 2000 and 2010 that had never happened before in United States history.

The first came with the presidential election of 2000. The winner wasn't decided until more than a month after the election!

The Democratic candidate was Al Gore, who had served as Bill Clinton's vice president. The Republican candidate was George W. Bush, whose father, George H. W. Bush, had been the president Clinton had replaced in 1992. The race was a tight one, but no one expected what happened on election night. At first it looked like Al Gore had won. Then it seemed George Bush had won. It came down to the state of Florida. Which candidate would take the state of Florida's twenty-five electoral votes? Whoever won Florida would win the election and become president. By early the next morning, only about 2,000 votes throughout the whole state separated the candidates.

Neither Bush nor Gore wanted to concede. That means they wouldn't give up or give in. When a vote is that close, by law the state must conduct a recount. At the time the recount started, Bush's lead had dwindled to about 900 votes. What happened next can only be described as a big mess. There were questions about which ballots to count and whether the ballots should be counted by hand—and, if so, what the counters should look for. Sometimes it wasn't clear by looking at the ballot whether Gore or Bush was intended to get the vote. Time limits were imposed on the counting and then changed by the courts.

Finally, on December 12, thirty-five days after the election, the U.S. Supreme Court halted the counting, which effectively gave Florida's electoral votes—and the presidency—to George Bush.

Then in 2001, terror and tragedy struck the United States. On September 11, 2001, nineteen men belonging to the terrorist group al-Qaeda hijacked four commercial airplanes. They crashed two of the planes into New York City's Twin Towers at the World Trade Center. The towers, two of the best-known landmarks in the country, collapsed within hours. A third airplane was crashed into the Pentagon, the home of the Department of Defense in Washington, D.C. On a fourth plane, the passengers, who had already been alerted about the other terrorist attacks, tried to take back the plane as the hijackers also headed to Washington.

They caused the plane to crash in a field in Pennsylvania. As on the other planes, everyone aboard died, but the crew and passengers were hailed as heroes for preventing another attack on the nation's capital.

The attacks—the first such on U.S. soil—resulted in the loss of almost three thousand lives and cost billions of dollars in lost jobs and business and also in cleanup. There is no way to measure the toll the attacks took on the lives of the friends and families of the victims, on the first responders, and on the national spirit.

Another result of the attacks was war. The terrorist organization al-Qaeda, led by Osama bin Laden, used training camps in Afghanistan to launch their attacks. President George Bush decided, a little less than a month after September 11, to invade Afghanistan. Most Americans supported his decision. The war to free the country from an Afghan government that supported al-Qaeda morphed into a costly struggle that went on for more than a decade.

In 2003, President Bush ordered the U.S. military to invade another Middle Eastern country. This time it was Iraq—the same country his father had attacked over a decade earlier. Iraq had nothing to do with the events of September 11, but the Bush administration insisted that Iraq had weapons of mass destruction and that the regime of Iraq's dictator, Saddam Hussein, must be overthrown. Other countries agreed to fight alongside the United States, but the war was controversial, both inside and outside the U.S. The Iraq war began on March 20, 2003. The struggle was long and costly in both money and lives. No weapons of mass destruction were ever found. American soldiers left Iraq in 2011, leaving behind a fragile government.

The presidential election of 2008 brought another first for the United States. Barack Obama, a Democratic senator from Illinois, beat the Republican candidate, Senator John McCain of Arizona, to become the first African American president of the United States. But before Barack Obama won, he had to first secure the right to be the Democrats' candidate. To do that, he had to do battle with a strong, tenacious contender who wanted to become the first woman president of the United States. She was a senator from the state of New York, and her name was Hillary Clinton.

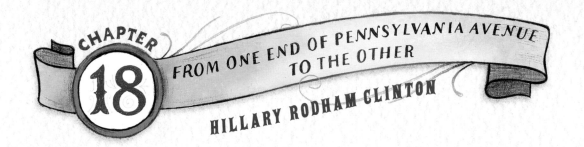

HILLARY RODHAM CLINTON

The White House, where the president and his family live, sits at 1600 Pennsylvania Avenue. If you walk 1.2 miles east, you'll get to the Capitol Building, which houses Congress. Both of those buildings have been important to Hillary Clinton.

Hillary Clinton moved into the White House with her husband and their twelve-year-old daughter, Chelsea, after Bill Clinton won the presidency in the 1992 election and was inaugurated in 1993.

Her time in the White House was tough. Like most first ladies, she hoped to spend her days doing good for the country. One thing Mrs. Clinton wanted was to see that more Americans had access to health care. President Clinton knew his wife was a smart lawyer who was passionate about causes she felt would make the United States a better place to live. He appointed her to work on health care reform, even though some people thought a first lady should not be involved in making government policy. Mrs. Clinton worked hard on health care, but many inside and outside government worked just as hard against her plan, and it never came to a congressional vote.

During President Clinton's first term in office, some people also suggested she and the president had been involved in an illegal real estate deal back in Arkansas, where President Clinton had served as governor. This affair was known as Whitewater, the name of

HILLARY RODHAM CLINTON

the parcel of land in question. Investigations were launched, but no wrongdoing was ever proved.

In 1998, during her husband's second term, Hillary Clinton found herself in the middle of a devastating personal scandal not of her making. President Clinton was discovered to have been involved with a young woman, an intern at the White House, and was accused of lying about the affair.

Hillary Clinton was humiliated. She thought about divorcing her husband. Instead, she decided that she was going to remake her life on her terms. President Clinton's time in office would be up soon. What did she want to do with the rest of *her* life?

When it was first suggested to her that she run for the open Senate seat in New York, Mrs. Clinton was skeptical. For one thing, she didn't live in New York, though she and President Clinton had considered moving there after they left the White House.

The more she thought about it, however, Hillary Clinton saw that a run for the Senate would be a chance to escape from her husband's shadow. If she won, she would be a powerful politician in her own right. First, though, she had to win.

As planned, she and President Clinton moved to Chappaqua, New York. After a hard-fought Senate race in 2000, Hillary Clinton won the New York seat by a comfortable margin. Many people expected Senator Clinton to hog the spotlight when she came to the Senate. Instead, she kept a low profile, learned her job, and forged relationships with both Democrats and Republicans.

After September 11, 2001, Hillary Clinton, as a senator from New York, was deeply involved in bringing financial and health aid to her constituents who had suffered from the attack.

She also worked on budget issues, and on health and education reform. In 2006, she decided to run for a second Senate term, but she was already thinking about a run for the presidency. In 2007, she posted an announcement on her website that she would make the presidential run. "I'm in, and I'm in to win," she told supporters.

The battle for the Democratic Party's nomination between Clinton and Barack Obama was one of the most exciting in presidential history, teetering back and forth with first one ahead, then the other. Whoever won would be a "first": either the first woman or the first African American to head a major party ticket. Then it would be on to the presidential race, and a chance to become the first female or black president.

Eventually, Barack Obama prevailed. After the nomination, he went on to win the general election to become the forty-fourth president of the United States. But during the long campaign for the Democratic nomination, President Obama came to greatly respect his rival. She was smart, hardworking, and tenacious—that means she wouldn't give up. When it came time to appoint a secretary of state, the person who would advise the president on foreign affairs and carry out international policies for the United States, President Obama chose Hillary Clinton.

CHAPTER 19 THE CHANGING SENATE

MARIA CANTWELL
KAY BAILEY HUTCHISON * MARY LANDRIEU
DEBORAH STABENOW * LISA MURKOWSKI
ELIZABETH DOLE

During the first decade of the twenty-first century, 2000–2010, the Senate of the United States had more woman members at one time than ever before. The number reached its highest point in the 109th Congress, 2005–2007: eighteen.

Does that sound like a lot? Eighteen women out of one hundred members is less than 20 percent of the Senate. Yet women make up a bit more than 50 percent of the population of the United States.

Still, there were things to cheer about. California and Maine were no longer the only states with two woman senators! In 2000, Senator Patty Murray of Washington was joined by another Democrat, Maria Cantwell. She was a businesswoman in the tech industry who had served one term as a representative in the U.S. House before embarking on her business career. In 2000, she won her Senate race after an extremely close election, winning by less than 1 percent. Reelected to the Senate in 2006 and 2012, Senator Cantwell's signature issues are energy independence and the environment, no surprise since Washington prides itself on its pristine air and water and is nicknamed the Evergreen State.

The Wilderness Society has described Maria Cantwell as an "environmental champion."

The women who served in the U.S. Senate during the first decade of the twenty-first century were a varied group. Some, like Kay Bailey Hutchison from Texas, leaned conservative. Others, like Deborah Stabenow from Michigan, leaned liberal. Mary Landrieu came from Louisiana, in the deep South, while Lisa Murkowski was born and raised way, way up north in Alaska. But the senators also

MARIA CANTWELL

had things in common. These women were well educated, and many had served in local or national government before coming to the Senate.

KAY BAILEY HUTCHISON

DEBORAH STABENOW

MARY LANDRIEU

LISA MURKOWSKI

There was another senator who, like Hillary Clinton, had experience with presidential politics. Republican Elizabeth Dole served in two presidents' cabinets. She was secretary of transportation under President Ronald Reagan, and she served as secretary of labor in the cabinet of the first President Bush. In 1996, her husband, Senator Bob Dole from Kansas, ran for president against Hillary Clinton's husband, President Bill Clinton. Had he won, Liddy Dole would have been first lady. Instead, in 2000 Elizabeth Dole decided she'd run for president herself. Before the campaign really got under way, though, she had to drop out of the race because she hadn't raised enough money.

In 2002, a Senate seat opened in her home state of North Carolina. Mrs. Dole ran and won. Her husband, a former U.S. Senate majority leader, was out of the Senate when Mrs. Dole took her seat in 2003. She served one term.

Just as in the Senate, the number of women on the other side of Congress, the House of Representatives, was rising during the first decade of the new millennium.

And one woman was making her way up the ladder to its most important job: speaker of the House.

ELIZABETH DOLE

CHAPTER 20

MADAME SPEAKER
NANCY PELOSI

The speaker of the House of Representatives is one of the most important positions in the United States government. The position is established in Article I, Section 2 of the Constitution. The speaker is elected on the first day of every new Congress from the party that holds the most seats in the House (the majority party; the party with fewer seats is the minority). If the president should die in office, the vice president takes his place. Next in line is the speaker of the House.

What does the speaker do? Besides representing the district from which he or she was elected, the speaker works to get bills through the House that move forward the majority's agenda. A speaker has to have great legislative skills and know how to work with all the members of the House, Democrats and Republicans. Since 1789, fifty-three people have held the position of speaker of the House. Only one of them has been a woman: Nancy Pelosi.

NANCY PELOSI

Nancy D'Alesandro grew up in Baltimore, Maryland, the youngest child of a political family. After marrying Paul Pelosi, she moved to San Francisco, California, where she became active in Democratic politics. In 1987, after the youngest of her five children was in high school, Nancy Pelosi won a seat in the U.S. House of Representatives. Nancy was on her way to Washington.

Representative Pelosi worked her way up to becoming one of the Democratic Party leaders in the House. In 2002, when the Republicans controlled the House and the Democrats were in the minority, she became the minority leader. Then, in 2007, control of the House went back to the Democrats when they won the most seats in the 2006 election. Now the House needed a new speaker, and its Democratic members chose Nancy Pelosi.

Have you ever heard the term "glass ceiling"? It's an invisible barrier that women hit when they try to rise in their jobs. It's called glass because sometimes women don't know it's there until they hit it. Nancy Pelosi felt that by being elected speaker of the House, she not only broke through a glass ceiling, she smashed through a substance much harder: the ceiling of government, which has always put limits on women.

Nancy Pelosi took the speaker's gavel for the first time on January 4, 2007. Proud and honored, she said this:

"It is an historic moment for the Congress, and an historic moment for the women of this country. It is a moment for which we have waited for over 200 years. Never losing faith, we waited through the many years of struggle to achieve our rights. But women weren't just waiting; women were working. Never losing faith, we worked to redeem the promise of America, that all men and women are created equal. For our daughters and granddaughters, today we have broken the marble ceiling. For our daughters and granddaughters, the sky is the limit. Anything is possible for them."

WHAT GOES MUST

Female members of the House of Representatives standing on the steps of the U.S. Capitol prior to the official opening of the 113th Congress, 2013.

I n 2010, the Democrats lost control of the House of Representatives. That means there were more Republicans elected than Democrats, so they became the majority party. Nancy Pelosi, although still a member of Congress, would no longer be speaker of the House because she was a Democrat. The Republicans chose a man, John Boehner, to replace her.

There was another consequence to the 2010 election. The number of women in Congress has never been high, but it did creep up over the decades. Then, after the 2010 election, something happened for the first time since 1978. Fewer women were going to be serving in Congress.

Before the 2010 election, there were ninety woman representatives and senators.

After the election, eighty-seven women won their elections to serve in the 112th Congress, three fewer women than had served in the 111th.

Maybe that doesn't seem like a big deal. But for decades it had been taken for granted that the number of women in Congress would always go up. Now it seemed what goes up can go down, too.

In 2011, several women in Congress were in the news. For one, Democratic representative Gabrielle Giffords, the reason was tragic.

Known as Gabby, Giffords was one of the most popular members of the U.S. House. She came to Washington in 2007 after serving in both the Arizona House and Senate. She was a Democrat, but she knew how to get along with Republican House members. No matter their party, representatives responded to her friendliness and bright smile.

On January 8, 2011, Giffords was at a store near Tucson, meeting her constituents, the folks she represented in Congress. She was always interested in what voters had to say, so she organized local forums called "Congress on Your Corner." While she was shaking hands and answering questions, a man named

Jared Loughner ran up to her, a gun in his hand. He began firing over and over into the crowd. Nineteen people were injured; six of them, including a nine-year-old girl, died. Gabrielle Giffords was shot in the head.

An intern working for Giffords gave her first aid, and when help arrived, she was taken to the University Medical Center of Tucson in critical condition. It was touch-and-go as to whether she would live—and if so, what kind of life would she have?

Giffords's husband, astronaut Mark Kelly, said she would have a rough road ahead, and she did. But with excellent medical care, in Tucson and at Houston's Texas Medical Center, and thanks to her own unrelenting dedication to her recovery, Gabby pulled through, regaining the ability to walk, talk, and read, though still with many impediments.

Gabrielle Giffords hoped to return to her seat in Congress, but on January 22, 2012, she resigned, knowing that the voters she represented needed a full-time congressperson and that she needed more time to heal.

On January 25, she came to the House to submit her resignation. Her fellow House members burst into cheers and gave her a standing ovation. At that time, there was little that Republicans and Democrats agreed upon, but they did agree about this: Gabby Giffords was an inspiration, and everyone hoped she would fulfill her wish—to be reelected to the House and return to Congress once more as a U.S. representative from the state of Arizona.

Two other congresswomen made news in 2011:

GABRIELLE GIFFORDS

Republican representative Michele Bachmann from Minnesota and Maine senator Olympia Snowe. One was in the headlines because she wanted to play a more prominent role in government, the other because she wanted to give up her seat.

Michele Bachmann, a conservative Republican representative from Minnesota, decided in 2011 that she wanted to make a run to be her party's nominee for president. She received early support, especially in Iowa, where she won the state's straw poll as the candidate participants wanted to see as the Republican nominee. She also took part in several presidential debates with other Republican nominees. But her support waned, and by January 2012, she suspended her campaign.

Maine's senator Olympia Snowe, after three six-year terms in the Senate, decided it was time to retire. It wasn't that she thought she couldn't win. In fact, she was sure she could. But since she had arrived in the Senate, in 1994, Congress had become more and more partisan. Republicans and Democrats, despite their many differences, used to be able to come together for the good of the country. By 2012, that rarely happened.

As Senator Snowe said in her resignation letter: "I do find it frustrating . . . that an atmosphere of polarization and 'my way or the highway' ideologies has become pervasive in campaigns and in our governing institutions." She added: "Unfortunately, I do not realistically expect the partisanship of recent years in the Senate to change over the short term."

* * * * * * *

If supporters of women in Congress had felt dejected after the 2010 election, in 2012 they once more had something to cheer! It was a record-breaking year for woman candidates.

The 113th Congress welcomed twenty woman senators! Twenty senators, one-fifth of the 100-member body. The most women in Senate history!

Along with returning senators, there were five freshmen: Republican Deb Fischer (Nebraska) and Democrats Mazie Hirono (Hawaii), Elizabeth Warren (Massachusetts), Heidi Heitkamp (North Dakota), and Tammy Baldwin (Wisconsin). Tammy Baldwin is the first openly gay U.S. senator, and Mazie Hirono is the first Asian American female senator. Warren, Baldwin, and Hirono also are the first woman senators elected from their states.

The election results were equally impressive in the House of Representatives. There were eighty women in the House, up from fifty-three in the previous Congress. Though they made up only 17.9 percent of the House,

DEB FISCHER

MAZIE HIRONO

ELIZABETH WARREN

HEIDI HEITKAMP

TAMMY BALDWIN

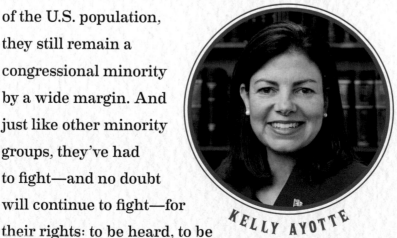

TAMMY DUCKWORTH

this freshman class had the most incoming women since 1992's Year of the Woman. Sixty-one of the woman representatives were Democrats, nineteen were Republicans. Notably, two of the new members were military veterans, including Illinois representative Tammy Duckworth, who lost both her legs while serving in Iraq.

One other notable accomplishment occurred in New Hampshire. Two newly elected woman representatives— Ann McLane Kuster and Carol Shea-Porter— joined New Hampshire's two female senators—Kelly Ayotte and Jeanne Shaheen—making the state the first to ever send an all-woman delegation to Washington. New Hampshire also had elected a female governor: Maggie Hassan.

Despite these great advancements, it's still worth noting that while women make up about half of the U.S. population, they still remain a congressional minority by a wide margin. And just like other minority groups, they've had to fight—and no doubt will continue to fight—for their rights: to be heard, to be

ANN McLANE KUSTER

CAROL SHEA-PORTER

KELLY AYOTTE

JEANNE SHAHEEN

accepted, to be respected. Woman representatives didn't even have their own private bathroom in the House until 1993!

There's an old, old saying—it goes back to the ancient Greeks: "A woman belongs in the home." That meant women should be in the house doing "women's work": cooking, cleaning, raising children. For centuries that's exactly where most women stayed.

Today, most American women have choices about how to spend their lives. They can be at home taking care of their families. They can also be out in the working world. Many, many women do both. For some of those women, their work will be in political office, helping to shape and make the laws of the United States.

Each woman who has served in the United States Congress, even if she didn't consider herself an advocate for women's rights, has pushed the ball forward just by taking her seat in the halls of government. The presence of women has changed the way our country works and the way the United States sees itself.

THERE'S NO DOUBT ABOUT IT:

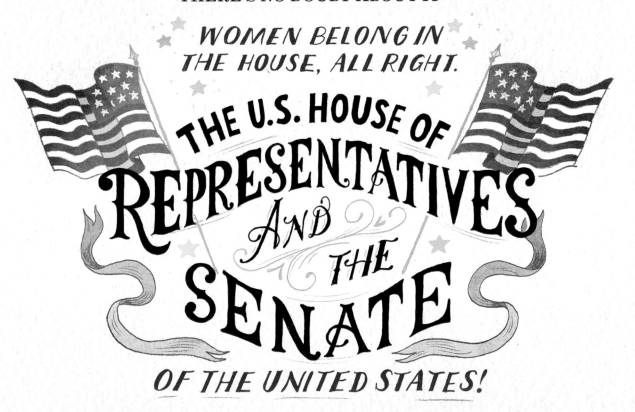

WOMEN BELONG IN THE HOUSE, ALL RIGHT. THE U.S. HOUSE OF REPRESENTATIVES AND THE SENATE OF THE UNITED STATES!

Certain terms, institutions, and procedures mentioned in the book are defined in this section, in the order in which they appear in the book.

* THE THREE BRANCHES OF GOVERNMENT
* WOMAN SUFFRAGE
* POLITICS AND POLITICIANS
* DEMOCRATS AND REPUBLICANS
* HOW A BILL IS PASSED
* CONGRESSIONAL COMMITTEES
* THE CABINET
* THE WOMEN'S MOVEMENT
* THE EQUAL RIGHTS AMENDMENT
* IMPEACHMENT

THE THREE BRANCHES OF GOVERNMENT

When the Founding Fathers wrote the U.S. Constitution, they wanted to form a strong national government that would still protect the rights of its citizens as well as the rights of individual states.

One of the ways they accomplished this was by dividing the government into three separate branches: legislative, executive, and judicial. This separation means the rights and responsibilities of each branch checks and balances the other two.

The legislative branch of the United States government is called the Congress. It has two "bodies," or chambers, the House of Representatives and the Senate.

The House of Representatives (often simply called the House) is made up of 435 representatives from the states. The number of representatives each state sends to Washington, D.C., the home of our nation's government, depends on population, but every state must have at least one representative. So California, the most populated state, has the most representatives. Alaska is large in area but small in population. It has one representative. (Until 1911, the House membership increased with population increases, but it's been at 435 since then, and the size of the district is what changes.)

Because the writers of the Constitution wanted the House of Representatives to be closest to its voters, House members serve for a two-year term. Then they have to go home and ask voters to reelect them. The makeup of the Senate is not based on population. Every state, big or small, gets two senators. With fifty states in the union, that means the Senate has one hundred members. Senators serve for six-year terms. Only one-third of senators come up for reelection every two years.

General elections for both bodies of Congress are held on the first Tuesday after the first Monday in November of even-numbered years, but the newly elected officials do not start serving until the following January.

The leader of the House of Representatives is called the speaker of the House and is always a member of the party that has the most members, or the majority. The speaker has a powerful job. He or she can decide what bills come before the House, who gets called upon to speak in debates, and who will be chosen to serve on committees looking into legislation that might become law.

The speaker of the House, who usually does not participate in debates or votes, is helped by another leader of his or her party, the majority leader. The minority leader heads the party that has fewer members.

The presiding officer of the Senate is the vice president of the United States, and he or she is given that duty by the Constitution. However, except in the case of a tie, the vice president cannot vote on any bills or issues that come before the Senate. The real power in the Senate belongs to the majority and minority leaders. The majority leader of the Senate is similar to the speaker of the House, with the power to see what legislation will be pushed forward and who will serve on committees.

It is Congress's job to make the laws that govern the United States. It decides how tax money will be spent. It can conduct investigations into foreign policy and domestic activities. It has the power to confirm presidential appointments and ratify treaties. It is supposed to be Congress's job to declare wars, but recent presidents have found ways to get around this role that belongs to Congress.

The executive branch of the U.S. government is led by the president of the United States. He (so far, it has never been a she) is the head of state, the face of the American government. With his party's leaders in Congress, he sets the agenda for the country: what issues we will focus on. It is the president who meets with other heads of governments and foreign dignitaries. The president is the commander in chief of the armed forces. It is also part of the president's responsibility to appoint ambassadors to other countries and negotiate trade agreements.

Should something interfere with the president's ability to do his job, it passes to the vice president.

The president also has an important role in passing legislation. He must agree to the laws Congress passes. If he does not want to sign a bill, he can say no—or veto it. Congress can try again. If it gets a two-thirds majority, it can override the president's veto.

Another part of the executive branch is the president's cabinet. These men and women help the president run the government so that it performs efficiently. Today there are fifteen heads of agencies that make up the cabinet, and many of them are called secretaries. The attorney general is also in the cabinet.

The president and vice president are elected as one unit and serve a four-year term. If they run for reelection and win, they are given another four-year term, but a president cannot serve more than two terms. Presidential elections are held in every year divisible by four, on the first Tuesday after the first Monday in November, at the same time as congressional elections.

The Supreme Court of the United States is the highest court in the land and makes up the judicial branch. Nine judges sit on the Supreme

Court and may hold their jobs for life. They are appointed by the president and confirmed by the Senate.

The Supreme Court interprets the laws of the United States. It may overrule decisions made by lower courts, and it can decide if laws coming from Congress or decisions made by the president are unconstitutional—going against something written in the U.S. Constitution.

WOMAN SUFFRAGE

Woman suffrage is the term for the long battle to get women the right to vote.

The first women's rights convention was held in Seneca Falls, New York, during the summer of 1848. The gathering sprang from an idea five women had while drinking tea in the home of Jane Hunt. Lucretia Mott, a Quaker preacher; her sister, Martha Wright; and Mary Ann McClintock listened as Elizabeth Cady Stanton, who had been active in reform movements such as the abolition of slavery, complained she was unable to use her talents now that she had assumed the traditional roles of wife and mother.

As the group talked more about the injustices against women, they decided to do something about it—which in those days often meant holding a convention; this one would be centered on women's rights. Their main point was made clear in their Declaration of Independence. "We hold these truths to be self-evident: that all men and women are created equal."

The convention became a popular annual event. At one of them, Stanton met Susan B. Anthony. Anthony could see how valuable it would be to all reform movements, including the abolition of slavery, if women had the right to vote. They could then elect politicians who would represent their beliefs and champion their causes.

Susan B. Anthony combined her considerable organizational talents with those of Elizabeth Cady Stanton, who spoke and wrote with passion. They fought for women's rights, including suffrage, for almost sixty years. They were surrounded by many other women pushing voting rights forward.

In 1871, some people claimed that women were already granted the right to vote by the Fourteenth and Fifteenth Amendments to the U.S. Constitution, which afforded the protections of the Constitution to all citizens. The focus of the amendments was on males, but that didn't stop some women from attempting to cast a ballot; they were turned away or their votes were not counted. Susan B. Anthony voted in 1872 and was put on trial for violating election laws. She lost, and the case was structured in such a way she was not able to appeal it to the Supreme Court.

A similar case in 1874 reached the Supreme Court, which ruled that the Constitution did not grant suffrage to anyone; that right was given to the states. All the Constitution could do was forbid discrimination on certain grounds through its amendments. Sex was not one of those grounds.

The decision by the Supreme Court meant there would be no easy way women could get the right to vote. They would have to continue the struggle in the territories and in the states. Individual states and territories, beginning in the last half of the nineteenth century, did allow women the vote. But it was not until 1920 that all women were granted that right through the states' adoption of the Nineteenth Amendment.

POLITICS AND POLITICIANS

Women and men elected to a government office are called politicians. Their office can be at the federal level (a president or senator), the state level (a governor or a state legislator), or the local level (a mayor or council member). Politics is the way officials govern, how they run the country, state, or city. Some politicians who build big political "machines" to do their will are called political bosses.

DEMOCRATS AND REPUBLICANS

There have been many political parties in U.S. history. Today there are two main ones: Democrats and Republicans.

A political party is a group of individuals who all want certain public policies enacted. The party puts forward candidates for elective office, and the candidates argue for these policies. Voters then decide which policies—which party—they prefer. Winning candidates work to put these polices into place once they are elected.

Though the views of the parties have sometimes changed on various issues over the years, in recent history the Republicans have been the more conservative party. They believe that government is not the solution to most issues. Democrats, considered more liberal, feel government can be a useful tool to help solve problems in the country. Parties do form in opposition to Democrats and Republicans but

traditionally have not gained much traction. There have been independent candidates, such as Ross Perot in 1992, who have made solid stabs at the presidency.

HOW A BILL IS PASSED

A bill is a proposed piece of legislation. The main job of Congress is to write, debate, and pass (or reject) new laws.

Congress meets during a legislative session to do its work. Each session of two years begins in an odd-numbered year after the general election held in November of an even-numbered year.

During the legislative session, members can write and introduce their own bills. Usually they will ask other members to sign their names to the bills they want to introduce and become the bills' cosponsors. The more cosponsors a bill has, the stronger its backing and likelihood of being passed.

The Congress is not the only place where ideas for bills originate. Government agencies such as the Defense Department and the Agriculture Department also have ideas for bills. Outside groups and individual voters can all suggest laws to their representatives.

A bill must be written in a special way. The bill is given a number, showing if it comes from the House or the Senate. Then it is summarized, so legislators and their staffs can get an overview of what the bill is about. The text of the bill then goes into more detail.

Once a bill is introduced by its sponsor, it is assigned to a relevant committee. The committee discusses it, perhaps calls expert witnesses, and makes changes it deems necessary. The bill could "die" or be defeated in committee. But if approved by the committee, the leader of the majority party can move the bill forward for debate by all the members of the chamber where it originated, either the House or Senate.

After a bill is debated on the chamber floor, it is voted upon. It can be approved, tabled (a decision postponed), defeated, or sent back to committee. If approved, it is then passed to the other chamber for review, debate, and a vote. Once both the House and Senate pass a bill, a "conference committee" made up of both senators and representatives works out any differences between the House and Senate versions, which must be identical. This is called a reconciliation. When that is achieved and the reconciled bill is passed by both bodies, the bill is sent to the president of the United States for his signature.

If the president approves of the bill, he signs it and it becomes law. If he does not sign it, he has vetoed the bill. Should the House and Senate decide they want the bill to pass against the president's wishes, they may vote again on the bill, and if it receives a two-thirds majority in the House and Senate, it becomes law, overriding the president's veto.

CONGRESSIONAL COMMITTEES

The Congress has many bills that come before it, and it must provide oversight in many areas of government. Before House members or senators can vote, they have to learn about the bills: what's in them and how they will affect their constituents and the country as a whole. Congress is also called upon to vote on other issues that are not in bills, such as approving of appointments. Since it is impossible for everyone to know everything about all the issues that come before Congress—defense, appropriations, agriculture, education, just to name a very few—the committee system was devised.

The House and the Senate each has its own set of committees. Once a bill is introduced into Congress, it is referred to the appropriate committee. It's the committee's job to study the bill and hold hearings about it, at which witnesses can testify.

How are committees chosen? The majority party begins the process. Often one party may "hold" one chamber, while the other is held by the opposite party. The majority party gets together—or "caucuses"—to decide which congresspeople will be on what committee and who will be the chair of each. Members who have been in Congress the longest get preference. Sometimes members are chosen to sit on committees because they have a particular interest or expertise in a subject or because the issue affects the district they represent. The minority party is then given seats. Each committee has both majority and minority members, in proportion to their party's strength in the chamber in question. Often the work of a committee is so wide-ranging, it is divided into subcommittees.

There are also a few joint committees. These contain members of both the House and the Senate. One of these is the committee that oversees the workings of the Library of Congress.

At present there are about two hundred committees and subcommittees. Sixteen of the committees are "standing," or permanent.

Among the most important ones are the House Ways and Means Committee, which writes tax laws; the Senate Homeland Security Committee; and the Senate Appropriations Committee, which decides how money is spent.

THE CABINET

The idea of a presidential cabinet is as old as the presidency itself. Article II, Section 2 of the U.S. Constitution discusses the role of presidential advisers. Currently the president's cabinet includes the vice president and the heads of fifteen executive departments. Except for the attorney general, the chief law enforcement officer of the United States, they are all called secretaries. The cabinet includes the attorney general and the secretaries of state, treasury, defense, interior, agriculture, commerce, labor, health and human services, housing and urban development, transportation, energy, education, veterans affairs, and homeland security.

THE WOMEN'S MOVEMENT

As women in the United States pushed for more rights, that push turned into a movement. Historians have divided the women's movement into three parts or "waves."

The first wave took place in the late nineteenth and early twentieth centuries. Women like Elizabeth Cady Stanton, Susan B. Anthony, Lucy Stone, and many others worked to make sure women could vote. The first wave ended after the passage of the Nineteenth Amendment, which gave women in the United States the right to vote.

Even though many individual women broke barriers and made strides during the entire twentieth century, the second wave of the women's movement did not get under way until the 1960s. The seeds of the second wave came in a 1963 book called *The Feminine Mystique* by Betty Friedan. The book touched many women who, like Friedan, were well-educated housewives who felt unfulfilled by the lives they were living. The second wave of the feminist movement was concerned with issues of equality in all walks of life: education, work, family, politics.

The third wave, which began in the 1980s, expanded the women's movement and included women of different races, sexualities, and cultural backgrounds, women who had different ways of seeing themselves than the less diverse women of the second wave.

The women's movement is the underlying force that has made it possible for women to have more equality, status, and choices throughout their lives.

THE EQUAL RIGHTS AMENDMENT

The words of the Equal Rights Amendment are plain: "Equality of rights under the law shall not be denied or abridged by the United States or by any state on account of sex."

The ERA, as it was called, meant that women, as well as men, had all the rights given by the U.S. Constitution. For instance, if the ERA was ratified, it would mean that women could not be discriminated against when it came to getting jobs or receiving the same wages as men for the same work.

The amendment goes on to say that Congress will have the power to enforce this amendment by making laws. It also says the amendment will take affect two years after ratification. That's the process by which states approve amendments to the United States Constitution.

But the Equal Rights Amendment was never ratified.

After any amendment is proposed in Congress, a supermajority of 66 $^2/_3$ percent in both the U.S. House of Representatives and the Senate must approve it. It then must be voted on by the states. This can be done by either the state legislatures or special state conventions, which must also vote overwhelmingly for the amendment—three-quarters of the states must vote in favor of an amendment for it to become law.

The Equal Rights Amendment was written in 1923 by Alice Paul, a lawyer and leader of the woman suffrage movement. It was introduced in Congress for almost fifty years. Finally, in 1972, the U.S. Congress moved the legislation on to the states for ratification. The ERA had a time limit of seven years in which it had to be passed by the states. Then the time limit was extended. But on June 30, 1982, the Equal Rights Amendment ran out of time. Only thirty-five states had ratified it, but it needed thirty-eight. Fifteen states did not. That meant the Equal Rights Amendment never became the law of the land.

IMPEACHMENT

Impeachment is the path by which certain high government officials are removed from office.

In Article II, Section 4, the U.S. Constitution says, "The President, Vice President and all civil officers of the United States, shall be removed from office on impeachment for, and conviction of, treason, bribery, or other high crimes and misdemeanors."

The Impeachment Clause, as it is called, raises several questions. Everyone knows who the President and Vice President are. But there has never been a definition of "civil officers." And unlike the commonly understood terms "treason" and "bribery," "high crimes and misdemeanors" has never been defined. In fact, in 1970 House Minority Leader (and future President) Gerald Ford said, "An impeachable offense is whatever a majority of the House of Representatives considers it to be at a given moment in history."

It is the House of Representatives that brings forth Articles of Impeachment. That means it is the House that makes the accusations of treason, bribery, or other high crimes. If a majority of the House votes to move the Articles forward, they are then presented to the Senate. It is the sole responsibility of the Senate to decide guilt or innocence.

There have been two presidents in U.S. history impeached by the House, Andrew Johnson in 1868 and Bill Clinton in 1998. Both men were acquitted by the Senate, and so they were not removed from office. President Richard Nixon, in 1974, resigned from office rather than face impeachment.

COMPLETE LIST OF WOMEN IN CONGRESS

Name		Chamber	State	Years	Name		Chamber	State	Years
Abel, Hazel Hempel		S	NE	1953-55	Carson, Julia May		H	IN	1997-2009
Abzug, Bella Savitzky		H	NY	1971-77	Castor, Kathy		H	FL	2007-
Adams, Sandra		H	FL,	2011-13	Chenoweth-Hage, Helen P.		H	ID	1995-2001
Allen, Maryon Pittman		S	AL	1977-79	Chisholm, Shirley Anita		H	NY	1969-83
Andrews, Elizabeth Bullock		H	AL	1971-73	Christensen, Donna Marie		D	VIRGIN ISL.	1997-
Ashbrook, Jean Spencer		H	OH	1981-83	Chu, Judy		H	CA	2009-
Ayotte, Kelly		S	NH	2011-	Church, Marguerite Stitt		H	IL	1951-63
Bachmann, Michele		H	MN	2007-	Clarke, Marian Williams		H	NY	1933-35
Baker, Irene Bailey		H	TN	1963-65	Clarke, Yvette Diane		H	NY	2007-
Baldwin, Tammy		H/S	WI	1999-	Clayton, Eva M.		H	NC	1991-2003
Bass, Karen		H	CA	2011-	Clinton, Hillary Rodham		S	NY	2001-09
Bean, Melissa L.		H	IL	2005-11	Collins, Barbara-Rose		H	MI	1991-97
Beatty, Joyce		H	OH	2013-	Collins, Cardiss		H	IL	1973-97
Bentley, Helen Delich		H	MD	1985-95	Collins, Susan Margaret		S	ME	1997-
Berkley, Shelley		H	NV	1999-2013	Cubin, Barbara L.		H	WY	1995-2009
Biggert, Judy Borg		H	IL	1999-2013	Dahlkemper, Kathleen A. (Kathy)		H	PA	2009-11
Black, Diane		H	TN	2011-	Danner, Patsy Ann (Pat)		H	MO	1993-2001
Blackburn, Marsha		H	TN	2003-	Davis, Jo Ann		H	VA	2001-09
Blitch, Iris Faircloth		H	GA	1955-63	Davis, Susan A.		H	CA	2001-
Boggs, Corinne Claiborne (Lindy)		H	LA	1973-91	DeGette, Diana		H	CO	1997-
Boland, Veronica Grace		H	PA	1941-43	DeLauro, Rosa L.		H	CT	1991-
Bolton, Frances Payne		H	OH	1939-69	Delbene, Susan K.		H	WA	2011-
Bonamici, Suzanne		H	OR	2011-	Dole, Elizabeth Hanford		S	NC	2003-09
Bono Mack, Mary		H	CA	1997-2013	Douglas, Emily Taft		H	IL	1945-47
Bordallo, Madeleine		D	GUAM	2003-	Douglas, Helen Gahagan		H	CA	1945-51
Bosone, Reva Zilpha Beck		H	UT	1949-53	Drake, Thelma D.		H	VA	2005-09
Bowring, Eva Kelly		S	NE	1953-55	Duckworth, Tammy		H	IL	2013-
Boxer, Barbara		H/S	CA	1983-	Dunn, Jennifer Blackburn		H	WA	1993-2005
Boyda, Nancy		H	KS	2007-09	Dwyer, Florence Price		H	NJ	1957-73
Brooks, Susan		H	IN	2013-	Edwards, Donna F.		H	MD	2007-
Brown, Corrine		H	FL	1993-	Edwards, Elaine Schwartzenburg		S	LA	1971-73
Brown-Waite, Virginia (Ginny)		H	FL	2003-11	Ellmers, Renee		H	NC	2011-
Brownley, Julia		H	CA	2013-	Emerson, Jo Ann		H	MO	1995-
Buchanan, Vera Daerr		H	PA	1951-57	English, Karan		H	AZ	1993-95
Buerkle, Ann Marie		H	NY	2011-13	Eshoo, Anna Georges		H	CA	1993-
Burdick, Jocelyn Birch		S	ND	1991-93	Eslick, Willa McCord Blake		H	TN	1931-33
Burke, Yvonne Brathwaite		H	CA	1973-79	Esty, Elizabeth		H	CT	2013-
Burton, Sala Galante		H	CA	1983-89	Fallin, Mary		H	OK	2007-11
Bushfield, Vera Cahalan		S	SD	1947-49	Farrington, Mary Elizabeth Pruett		D	HI	1953-57
Bustos, Cheri		H	IL	2013-	Feinstein, Dianne		S	CA	1991-
Byrne, Leslie Larkin		H	VA	1993-95	Felton, Rebecca Latimer		S	GA	1921-23
Byron, Beverly Barton Butcher		H	MD	1979-93	Fenwick, Millicent Hammond		H	NJ	1975-83
Byron, Katharine Edgar		H	MD	1941-43	Ferraro, Geraldine Anne		H	NY	1979-85
Cantwell, Maria E.		H/S	WA	1993-	Fiedler, Bobbi		H	CA	1981-87
Capito, Shelley Moore		H	WV	2001-	Fischer, Debra (Deb)		S	NE	2013-
Capps, Lois		H	CA	1997-	Fowler, Tillie Kidd		H	FL	1993-2001
Caraway, Hattie Wyatt		S	AR	1931-45	Foxx, Virginia Ann		H	NC	2005-
Carnahan, Jean		S	MO	2001-03	Frahm, Sheila		S	KS	1995-97

S—SENATE   H/S—TERMS IN BOTH HOUSE AND SENATE
H—HOUSE   BLUE—DEMOCRAT
D—DELEGATE   RED—REPUBLICAN

NOTE: DATES SHOWN ARE ACTUAL TERM(S) OF CONGRESS IN WHICH
THE INDIVIDUAL SERVED. IN SOME INSTANCES, THE REPRESENTATIVE,
SENATOR, OR DELEGATE ARRIVED AFTER THE START OF THE TERM OR
LEFT BEFORE ITS CONCLUSION.

Frankel, Lois	H	FL	2013–		Jordan, Barbara Charline	H	TX	1973–79
Fudge, Marcia L.	H	OH	2007–		Kahn, Florence Prag	H	CA	1925–37
Fulmer, Willa Lybrand	H	SC	1943–45		Kaptur, Marcia Carolyn (Marcy)	H	OH	1983–
Furse, Elizabeth	H	OR	1993–99		Kassebaum, Nancy Landon	S	KS	1977–97
Gabbard, Tulsi	H	HI	2013–		Kee, Maude Elizabeth	H	WV	1951–65
Gasque, Elizabeth Hawley	H	SC	1937–39		Kelly, Edna Flannery	H	NY	1949–69
Gibbs, Florence Reville	H	GA	1939–41		Kelly, Sue W.	H	NY	1995–2007
Giffords, Gabrielle	H	AZ	2007–2013		Kennelly, Barbara Bailey	H	CT	1981–99
Gillibrand, Kirsten	H/S	NY	2007–		Keys, Martha Elizabeth	H	KS	1975–79
Granahan, Kathryn Elizabeth	H	PA	1955–63		Kilpatrick, Carolyn Cheeks	H	MI	1997–2011
Granger, Kay	H	TX	1997–		Kilroy, Mary Jo	H	OH	2009–11
Grasso, Ella Tambussi	H	CT	1971–75		Kirkpatrick, Ann	H	AZ	2009–11
Graves, Dixie Bibb	S	AL	1937–39					2013–
Green, Edith Starrett	H	OR	1955–75		Klobuchar, Amy	S	MN	2007–
Greene Waldholtz, Enid	H	UT	1995–97		Knutson, Coya Gjesdal	H	MN	1955–59
Greenway, Isabella Selmes	H	AZ	1933–37		Kosmas, Suzanne M.	H	FL	2009–11
Griffiths, Martha Wright	H	MI	1955–75		Kuster, Ann McLane	H	NH	2013–
Hagan, Kay	S	NC	2009–		Landrieu, Mary L.	S	LA	1997–
Hahn, Janice	H	CA	2011–		Langley, Katherine Gudger	H	KY	1927–31
Hall, Katie Beatrice	H	IN	1981–85		Lee, Barbara	H	CA	1997–
Halvorson, Deborah L.	H	IL	2009–11		Lincoln, Blanche Lambert	H/S	AR	1993–97
Hanabusa, Colleen	H	HI	2011–					1999–2011
Hansen, Julia Butler	H	WA	1959–75		Lloyd, Marilyn Laird	H	TN	1975–95
Harden, Cecil Murray	H	IN	1949–59		Lofgren, Zoe	H	CA	1995–
Harman, Jane L.	H	CA	1993–99		Long, Catherine Small	H	LA	1985–87
			2001–13		Long, Jill Lynette	H	IN	1989–95
Harris, Katherine	H	FL	2003–07		Long, Rose McConnell	S	LA	1935–37
Hart, Melissa A.	H	PA	2001–07		Lowey, Nita M.	H	NY	1989–
Hartzler, Vicky	H	MO	2011–		Luce, Clare Boothe	H	CT	1943–47
Hawkins, Paula	S	FL	1979–87		Lujan Grisham, Michelle	H	NM	2013–
Hayworth, Nan	H	NY	2011–13		Lummis, Cynthia M.	H	WY	2009–
Heckler, Margaret M.	H	MA	1967–83		Lusk, Georgia Lee	H	NM	1947–49
Heitkamp, Mary Kathryn (Heidi)	S	ND	2013–		Majette, Denise L.	H	GA	2003–05
Herrera Beutler, Jaime	H	WA	2011–		Maloney, Carolyn Bosher	H	NY	1993–
Herseth Sandlin, Stephanie	H	SD	2003–11		Mankin, Helen Douglas	H	GA	1945–47
Hicks, Louise Day	H	MA	1971–73		Margolies-Mezvinsky, Marjorie	H	PA	1993–95
Hirono, Mazie	H/S	HI	2007–		Markey, Betsy	H	CO	2009–11
Hochul, Kathleen C.	H	NY	2011–13		Martin, Lynn Morley	H	IL	1981–91
Holt, Marjorie Sewell	H	MD	1973–87		Matsui, Doris Okada	H	CA	2005–
Holtzman, Elizabeth	H	NY	1973–81		May, Catherine Dean	H	WA	1959–71
Honeyman, Nan Wood	H	OR	1937–39		McCarthy, Carolyn	H	NY	1997–
Hooley, Darlene	H	OR	1997–2009		McCarthy, Karen	H	MO	1995–2005
Horn, Joan Kelly	H	MO	1991–93		McCaskill, Claire	S	MO	2007–
Huck, Winnifred Sprague Mason	H	IL	1921–23		McCollum, Betty	H	MN	2001–
Humphrey, Muriel Buck	S	MN	1977–79		McCormick, Ruth Hanna	H	IL	1929–31
Hutchison, Kathryn Ann Bailey (Kay)	S	TX	1993–2013		McKinney, Cynthia Ann	H	GA	1993–2003
Jackson Lee, Sheila	H	TX	1995–					2005–07
Jenckes, Virginia Ellis	H	IN	1933–39		McMillan, Clara Gooding	H	SC	1939–41
Jenkins, Lynn	H	KS	2009–		McMorris Rodgers, Cathy	H	WA	2005–
Johnson, Eddie Bernice	H	TX	1993–		Meek, Carrie P.	H	FL	1993–2003
Johnson, Nancy Lee	H	CT	1983–2007		Meng, Grace	H	NY	2013–
Jones, Stephanie Tubbs	H	OH	1999–2009		Meyers, Jan	H	KS	1985–97

Meyner, Helen Stevenson	H	NJ	1975–79	Sanchez, Loretta	H	CA	1997–
Mikulski, Barbara Ann	H/S	MD	1977–	Schakowsky, Janice D.	H	IL	1999–
Millender-McDonald, Juanita	H	CA	1995–2009	Schenk, Lynn	H	CA	1993–95
Miller, Candice S.	H	MI	2003–	Schmidt, Jean	H	OH	2005–13
Mink, Patsy Takemoto	H	HI	1965–77	Schneider, Claudine	H	RI	1981–91
			1989–2002	Schroeder, Patricia Scott	H	CO	1973–97
Molinari, Susan	H	NY	1989–99	Schwartz, Allyson Y.	H	PA	2005–
Moore, Gwendolynne S. (Gwen)	H	WI	2005–	Seastrand, Andrea	H	CA	1995–97
Morella, Constance A.	H	MD	1987–2003	Sekula Gibbs, Shelley	H	TX	2005–07
Moseley Braun, Carol	S	IL	1993–99	Sewell, Terri	H	AL	2011–
Murkowski, Lisa	S	AK	2001–	Shaheen, Jeanne	S	NH	2009–
Murray, Patty	S	WA	1993–	Shea-Porter, Carol	H	NH	2007–
Musgrave, Marilyn N.	H	CO	2003–09	Shepherd, Karen	H	UT	1993–95
Myrick, Sue	H	NC	1995–2013	Simpson, Edna Oakes	H	IL	1959–61
Napolitano, Grace Flores	H	CA	1999–	Sinema, Kyrsten	H	AZ	2013–
Negrete McLeod, Gloria	H	CA	2013–	Slaughter, Louise McIntosh	H	NY	1987–
Neuberger, Maurine Brown	S	OR	1959–67	Smith, Linda	H	WA	1995–99
Noem, Kristi	H	SD	2011–	Smith, Margaret Chase	H/S	ME	1939–73
Nolan, Mae Ella	H	CA	1921–25	Smith, Virginia Dodd	H	NE	1975–91
Norrell, Catherine Dorris	H	AR	1961–63	Snowe, Olympia Jean	H/S	ME	1979–2013
Northup, Anne Meagher	H	KY	1997–2007	Solis, Hilda L.	H	CA	2001–11
Norton, Eleanor Holmes	D	DC	1991–	Speier, Karen Lorraine Jacqueline	H	CA	2007–
Norton, Mary Teresa	H	NJ	1925–51	Spellman, Gladys Noon	H	MD	1975–81
O'Day, Caroline Love Goodwin	H	NY	1935–43	St. George, Katharine Price Collier	H	NY	1947–65
O'Loughlin McCarthy, Kathryn Ellen	H	KS	1933–35	Stabenow, Deborah Ann	H/S	MI	1997–
Oakar, Mary Rose	H	OH	1977–93	Stanley, Winifred Claire	H	NY	1943–45
Oldfield, Pearl Peden	H	AR	1927–31	Sullivan, Leonor Kretzer	H	MO	1953–77
Owen, Ruth Bryan	H	FL	1929–33	Sumner, Jessie	H	IL	1939–47
Patterson, Elizabeth J.	H	SC	1987–93	Sutton, Betty	H	OH	2007–13
Pelosi, Nancy	H	CA	1987–	Tauscher, Ellen O'Kane	H	CA	1997–2011
Pettis, Shirley Neil	H	CA	1975–79	Thomas, Lera Millard	H	TX	1965–67
Pfost, Gracie Bowers	H	ID	1953–63	Thompson, Ruth	H	MI	1951–57
Pingree, Chellie	H	ME	2009–	Thurman, Karen L.	H	FL	1993–2003
Pratt, Eliza Jane	H	NC	1945–47	Titus, Alice (Dina)	H	NV	2009–11
Pratt, Ruth Sears Baker	H	NY	1929–33				2013–
Pryce, Deborah D.	H	OH	1993–2009	Tsongas, Nicola S. (Niki)	H	MA	2007–
Pyle, Gladys	S	SD	1937–39	Unsoeld, Jolene	H	WA	1989–95
Rankin, Jeannette	H	MT	1917–19	Velázquez, Nydia M.	H	NY	1993–
			1941–43	Vucanovich, Barbara Farrell	H	NV	1983–97
Reece, Louise Goff	H	TN	1961–63	Wagner, Ann	H	MO	2013–
Reid, Charlotte Thompson	H	IL	1963–73	Walorski, Jackie	H	IN	2013–
Richardson, Laura	H	CA	2007–13	Warren, Elizabeth	S	MA	2013–
Riley, Corinne Boyd	H	SC	1961–63	Wasserman Schultz, Debbie	H	FL	2005–
Rivers, Lynn Nancy	H	MI	1995–2003	Waters, Maxine	H	CA	1991–
Robertson, Alice Mary	H	OK	1921–23	Watson, Diane Edith	H	CA	2001–11
Roby, Martha	H	AL	2011–	Weis, Jessica McCullough	H	NY	1959–63
Rogers, Edith Nourse	H	MA	1925–61	Wilson, Frederica	H	FL	2011–
Ros-Lehtinen, Ileana	H	FL	1989–	Wilson, Heather	H	NM	1997–2009
Roukema, Margaret Scafati	H	NJ	1981–2003	Wingo, Effiegene Locke	H	AR	1929–33
Roybal-Allard, Lucille	H	CA	1993–	Woodhouse, Chase Going	H	CT	1945–47
Saiki, Patricia Fukuda	H	HI	1987–91				1949–51
Sánchez, Linda T.	H	CA	2003–	Woolsey, Lynn C.	H	CA	1993–2013

◀ 121 ▶

ENDNOTES

Bibliographical information for print materials appears in the bibliography if it is not included here.

PART 1
"MEN, THEIR RIGHTS AND NOTHING MORE; WOMEN, THEIR RIGHTS AND NOTHING LESS"

page x The title of this part is taken from the motto of the journal *The Revolution*, published by Susan B. Anthony.

page 4 "This shall be . . .": quoted on www .theautry.org/explore/exhibits/suffrage.

❶ NUMBER ONE

page 5 The anecdote about Jeannette Rankin and her horse: in Gretchen Woelfle, *Jeannette Rankin: Political Pioneer*, p. 14.

page 6 "I may be . . .": quoted in Mallon, Winifred, "An Impression of Jeannette Rankin," *The Suffragist*, March 31, 1917, as cited on http://history.house.gov/People/Detail/20147?ret=True.

page 7 "old men . . .": See Norma Smith, *Jeannette Rankin: America's Conscience*, p. 99.

page 7 "I want to stand . . .": ibid, p. 104.

page 7 "a crying schoolgirl": quoted in Hannah Josephson, *Jeannette Rankin, First Lady of Congress: A Biography*, p. 77.

page 8 "By voting for me . . .": quoted in Jeannette Rankin, "Two Votes Against War and Other Writings on Peace." A. J. Muste Memorial Institute Pamphlet Essay Series, p. 11.

page 9 "No! As a woman . . .": quoted in Lynne E. Ford, *Encyclopedia of Women and American Politics*, p. 376.

page 9 "to be a worm" and "We are all human beings": quoted in Jeannette Rankin, "Two Votes," p. 12.

page 9 "Peace is a woman's job": ibid, p. 22.

❷ NEXT UP

page 11 "bartering the birthright . . .": quoted on http://history.house.gov/People/Detail/20480?ret=True.

page 11 "The farmers need . . .": ibid.

❸ WIDOWS (MOSTLY) . . .

page 16 "I made appointments . . .": quoted on http://history.house.gov/People/Detail/13054?ret=True.

page 17 "I pledge you . . .": quoted on www.findagrave.com/cgi-bin/fg.cgi?page=gr&GRid=9300.

page 19 "A capable woman . . .": quoted in "First Woman Named as House Chairman," *Washington Post*, December 14, 1923, as cited on http://history.house.gov/People/Detail/18986?ret=True.

page 20 "mother of the F.B.I.": quoted in Dorothy M. Brown, "Kahn, Florence Prag," *American National Biography*, New York: Oxford University Press, 1999, Volume 12, pp. 334–35, as cited on http://history.house.gov/People/Detail/16075?ret=True.

page 20 "like a man": "Pictorial Review" quoted in Hope Chamberlin, *A Minority of Members: Women in the U.S. Congress*, New York: Praeger, 1973, p. 50, as cited on http://history.house.gov/People/Detail/16075?ret=True.

page 20 "Sex appeal": quoted on: http://history.house.gov/People/Detail/16075?ret=True.

page 20 "Mrs. Kahn, shrewd . . .": Alice Roosevelt Longworth, "What Are the Women Up To?" *Ladies' Home Journal*, March 1934, p. 51, as cited on www.jwa.org/encyclopedia/article/kahn-florence-prag.

page 22 "I do not expect . . .": quoted in Suzanne O'Dea, *From Suffrage to the Senate: America's Political Women: An Encyclopedia of Leaders, Causes and Issues*, Volume I, p. 485.

page 22 "Battling Mary": http://history.house.gov/People/Detail/19024?ret=True.

page 22 "I'm prouder of . . .": ibid.

page 22 "I am no lady . . .": "Mary T. Norton," quoted in *Current Biography Yearbook*, 1944, New York: H. W. Wilson, p. 500, as cited on http://history.house.gov/People/Detail/19024?ret=True.

4 ... AND DAUGHTERS

page 24 "I have been ...": quoted in S. J. Woolf, "Mark Hanna's Daughter Chooses to Run," *New York Times* Sunday magazine, October 16, 1927, p. 10, as cited on http://history .house.gov/People/Detail/17791?ret=True.

page 25 "There are two ...": as quoted on www .thevoterupdate.com/articles/ 2009/11_10_09_mark_hanna.php.

page 25 "the Sweetheart of the House": quoted in Susan Tolchin, *Women in Congress 1917– 1976*, p. 89.

page 26 "the Spirit of Florida": quoted on: http://history.house.gov/People/ Detail/19256?ret=True.

page 27 "I did not turn ...": quoted in Susan Tolchin, *Women in Congress, 1917–1976*, p. 62, as cited on http://history.house.gov/People/ Detail/19256?ret=True.

5 THE WOMEN OF ARKANSAS

page 33 "The windows need ...": quoted in *Current Biography Yearbook, 1945*, New York: H. W. Wilson, 1945, p. 90, as cited on http://history.house.gov/People/ Detail/44589?ret=True.

page 33 "The time has passed ...": quoted in Susan M. Hartmann, "Caraway, Hattie Ophelia Wyatt," *American National Biography*, New York: Oxford University Press, 1999, Volume 4, pp. 369–70, as cited on http://history.house.gov/People/ Detail/44589?ret=True.

page 34 "I haven't the heart ...": quoted in *Current Biography*, as cited on http://history .house.gov/People/Detail/44589?ret=True.

page 35 "sweet privilege to serve ...": quoted in "Pro and Con," *Washington Post*, June 18, 1932, p. 6, as cited on: http://history.house .gov/People/Detail/23970?ret=True.

6 STARS!

page 38 "And you're not ...": quoted in Lynn Plourde, *Margaret Chase Smith: A Woman for President*, unpaged.

page 38 "selfish political exploitation": http:// www.infoplease.com/t/hist/declaration-of-conscience.

page 38 "The American people ...": www .mcslibrary.org/program/library/declaration .htm.

page 39 "When people keep telling you ...": quoted in Susan Tolchin, *Women in Congress*, p. 76, as cited on http://history.house.gov/ People/Detail/21866?ret=True.

page 40 "[M]en have decided ...": quoted in *Women Come to the Front: Journalists, Photographers, and Broadcasters During World War II*, Washington, D.C.: Library of Congress, 1995, as cited on http:// en.wikipedia.org/wiki/Clare_Boothe_Luce.

page 41 "She raised early ...": quoted in "Clare Boothe Luce, Renaissance Woman, Dies at 84," *Washington Post*, October 11, 1987, p. H6, as cited on http://history.house.gov/People/ Detail/17213?ret=True.

page 42 "I became active ...": quoted in Shirley Washington, *Outstanding Women Members of Congress*, p. 24, as cited on: http://history .house.gov/People/Detail/12399?ret=True.

page 42 "Politics is a job ...": quoted in Hope Chamberlin, *A Minority of Members: Women in the U.S. Congress*, p. 183, as cited on http://history.house.gov/People/ Detail/12399?ret=True.

page 43 "pink right down ...": quoted on http:// articles.latimes.com/1990-04-09/local/me-664_1_helen-gahagan-douglas.

PART 4
SETTLING DOWN AND STIRRING THINGS UP, 1954—1963

page 46 "Women can't be ...," "back into a corner," and "heartbreaking": quoted in Annabel Paxton, *Women in Congress*, p. 37; also Norton's obituary in *Current Biography Yearbook, 1969*, New York: H. W. Wilson, 1959, as cited on http://history .house.gov/Exhibitions-and-Publications/ WIC/Historical-Essays/National-Stage/ Legislative-Interests.

page 47 "At this rate ...": quoted in Marcy Kaptur, *Women of Congress: A Twentieth-Century Odyssey*, p. 65.

page 48 "the greatest demonstration for freedom ...": quoted on http://www.thekingcenter .org/archive/document/i-have-dream-1.

7 CARRYING THE BANNER

page 50 "If freedom has ...": quoted in Congressional Record, House, 86th Congress, March 11, 1960, p. 5316, as cited on: http://history.house.gov/People/ Detail/12556?ret=True.

page 50 "[I]f I can't take on ...": quoted in Marybeth Weston, "Ladies' Day on the Hustings," *New York Times* Sunday magazine, October 19, 1958, p. 32, as cited on ibid.

page 50 "they were sure ...": David Loth, *A Long Way Forward: The Biography of Congresswoman Frances Payne Bolton*, p. 289, as cited on: http://history.house.gov/People/ Detail/9566?ret=True.

page 51 "Negro Americans ...": quoted in Marcy Kaptur, *Women of Congress: A Twentieth-Century Odyssey*, p. 79.

page 51 "[Y]ou and I ...": quoted on http:// thisibelieve.org/essay/16387.

page 51 "If a man ...": quoted in Kerry Luft, "Marguerite Stitt Church, Ex-Congresswoman," *Chicago Tribune*, May 27, 1990, p. 8, as cited on: http://history.house .gov/People/Detail/10940?ret=True.

page 52 "a Kiddie Corps": quoted on http://history.house.gov/People/ Detail/10940?ret=True.

page 52 "Well": quoted in Marguerite Stitt Church, Oral History Interview, November 25, 1978, U.S. Association of Former Members of Congress, Manuscript Room, Library of Congress, Washington, D.C., pp. 28–30, as cited on http://history.house.gov/ People/Detail/10940?ret=True.

8 MISSOURI AND MICHIGAN

page 53 "We don't have ...": quoted in Susan Tolchin, *Women in Congress, 1917–1976*, p. 106, as cited on http://history.house.gov/ People/Detail/22444?ret=True.

page 54 "I saw my mother work ...": ibid, p. 121.

PART 5
"A CHANGE IS GONNA COME,"
1964–1979

page 57 The title of this part, "A Change Is Gonna Come," is taken from a song written by Sam Cooke in 1963.

9 A DIFFERENT KIND OF PIONEER

page 61 "stir up trouble": quoted on http://blog .hawaii.edu/aplpj/files/2011/11/APLPJ_04.2_ cruz.pdf.

page 62 "special burden" and "I always felt ...": Patsy T. Mink, Oral History Interview, March 6/March 26/June 7, 1979, U.S. Association of Former Members of Congress, Manuscript Room, Library of Congress, Washington, D.C., p. 74, as cited on http://history.house.gov/People/ Detail/18329?ret=True.

10 "UNBOUGHT AND UNBOSSED"

page 63 "You forget two things ...": quoted in Lucia Raatma, *Shirley Chisholm*, p. 24.

page 64 "immoral, unjust ...": ibid, p. 56.

page 64 "When I die ...": in *Shirley Chisholm '72: Unbought and Unbossed* (documentary film).

11 JOINING SHIRLEY

page 66 "Earlier today ..." and "Has the president ...": quoted on www .americanrhetoric.com/speeches/ barbarajordanjudiciarystatement.htm.

page 67 "In this election year ...": quoted on www.americanrhetoric.com/speeches/ barbarajordan1976dnc.html.

page 68 "When I walk ...": LaVerne McCain Gill, *African American Women in Congress*, p. 65.

12 TWO GOOD FRIENDS

page 69 "This woman's place": quoted on http://history.house.gov/People/ Detail/8276?ret=True.

page 70 "There are those ...": from Bella S. Abzug, *Bella! Ms. Abzug Goes to Washington*, as cited on http://en.wikiquote.org/wiki/ Bella_Abzug.

page 71 "Conscience of Congress": quoted in Amy Schapiro, *Millicent Fenwick: Her Way*, New Brunswick, N.J.: Rutgers University Press, 2003, p. 161, as cited on http://history.house.gov/People/Detail/13066?ret=True.

13 A WOMAN OF HER TIME

page 72 Touchdown Club incident: *New York Times*, January 23, 1996, www.nytimes.com/1996/01/23/style/chronicle-092584.html?ref=patricia_s_schroeder.

page 72 "over-aged frat house": quoted in Patricia Schroeder, *24 Years of House Work . . . and the Place Is Still a Mess*, as cited on http://history.house.gov/People/Detail/21313?ret=True.

page 73 "women and blacks . . .": quoted in Patricia Schroeder, *24 Years of House Work . . . and the Place Is Still a Mess*.

page 73 "Nobody else objected . . .": quoted in Patricia Schroeder, *24 Years of House Work . . . and the Place Is Still a Mess*.

page 74 "He told me . . ." and "He was a very good sport . . .": quoted in *New York Times* op. cit.

14 A POSSIBLE VICE PRESIDENT

page 75 "Finally, a tough Democrat": cited on http://history.house.gov/People/Detail/13081?ret=True.

15 PACIFIC STATE SENATOR, PRAIRIE STATE SENATOR

page 78 "A Fresh Face . . .": cited on http://history.house.gov/People/Detail/16096?ret=True.

16 THE YEAR OF THE WOMAN

page 88 "I am a fierce . . .": quoted on http://ros-lehtinen.house.gov/issue/foreign-affairs.

page 88 "Calling 1992 . . .": quoted on www.senate.gov/artandhistory/history/minute/year_of_the_woman.htm.

17 MAINE—TWO WOMAN SENATORS

page 89 "America's 10 Best Senators": *Time*, April 24, 2006, www.time.com/time/

magazine/article/0,9171,1184052-7,00.html.

page 90 "One of the highlights . . .": guest column, Lewiston, Maine, *Sun Journal*, October 14, 2007, www.sunjournal.com/node/744066.

18 FROM ONE END OF PENNSYLVANIA AVENUE TO THE OTHER

page 98 "I'm in, and I'm in to win": quoted on http://www.cnn.com/2007/POLITICS/01/20/clinton.announcement/index.html.

19 THE CHANGING SENATE

page 100 "environmental champion": quoted on http://www.opencongress.org/wiki/Maria_Cantwell.

20 MADAME SPEAKER

page 103 "It is an historic . . .": quoted on www.sfgate.com/bayarea/article/Text-of-Nancy-Pelosi-s-speech-2625996.php#page-2.

PART 8
WHAT GOES UP MUST COME DOWN— AND GOES BACK UP!

page 108 "I do find it frustrating . . .": quoted in *New York Times*, February 29, 2012, www.nytimes.com/2012/02/29/us/politics/snowe-opts-not-to-seek-re-election-in-maine.html?_r=0.

APPENDIX

IMPEACHMENT

page 118 "An impeachable offense . . .": http://en.wikipedia.org/wiki/Impeachment.

BIBLIOGRAPHY

BOOKS

Abzug, Bella S. *Bella! Ms. Abzug Goes to Washington.* Edited by Mel Ziegler. New York: Saturday Review Press, 1972.

Chamberlin, Hope. *A Minority of Members: Women in the U.S. Congress.* New York: Praeger, 1973.

Chisholm, Shirley. *Unbought and Unbossed.* Boston: Houghton Mifflin, 1970.

Clinton, Hillary Rodham. *Living History.* New York: Simon & Schuster, 2003.

Cooper, Ilene. *Susan B. Anthony.* New York: Franklin Watts, 1984.

Ford, Lynne E. *Encyclopedia of Women and American Politics.* New York: Facts on File, 2008.

Friedan, Betty. *The Feminine Mystique.* New York: Norton, 1963.

Gill, LaVerne McCain. *African American Women in Congress: Forming and Transforming History.* New Brunswick, N.J.: Rutgers University Press, 1997.

Hutchison, Kay Bailey. *Leading Ladies: American Trailblazers.* New York: HarperCollins, 2008.

*Josephson, Hannah. *Jeannette Rankin, First Lady of Congress: A Biography.* New York: Bobbs-Merrill, 1974.

Kaptur, Marcy. *Women of Congress: A Twentieth-Century Odyssey.* Washington D.C.: Congressional Quarterly, 1996.

*Krull, Kathleen. *A Woman for President: The Story of Victoria Woodhull.* Illus. by Jane Dyer. New York: Walker, 2004.

Loth, David. *A Long Way Forward: The Biography of Congresswoman Frances Payne Bolton.* New York: Longmans, Green, 1957.

Morris, Sylvia Jukes. *Rage for Fame: The Ascent of Clare Boothe Luce.* New York: Random House, 1997.

O'Dea, Suzanne. *From Suffrage to the Senate: America's Political Women: An Encyclopedia of Leaders, Causes and Issues.* Volumes I and II. Millerton, N.Y.: Grey House Publishing, 2006.

*suitable for young readers

Palmer, Barbara, and Dennis Simon. *Women and Congressional Elections: A Century of Change.* Boulder, Colo.: Lynne Rienner Publishers, 2012.

Paxton, Annabel. *Women in Congress,* Richmond, Va.: Deitz Press, 1945.

*Plourde, Lynn. *Margaret Chase Smith: A Woman for President.* Illus. by David McPhail. Watertown, Mass.: Charlesbridge, 2008.

*Raatma, Lucia. *Shirley Chisholm.* New York: Marshall Cavendish Benchmark, 2010.

Schapiro, Amy. *Millicent Fenwick: Her Way.* New Brunswick, N.J.: Rutgers University Press, 2003

Schroeder, Patricia. *24 Years of House Work . . . and the Place Is Still a Mess: My Life in Politics.* Kansas City, Mo.: Andrews McMeel, 1998.

Scobie, Ingrid Winther. *Center Stage: Helen Gahagan Douglas: A Life.* New York: Oxford University Press, 1992.

Sherman, Janann. *No Place for a Woman: A Life of Senator Margaret Chase Smith. (Rutgers Series on Women and Politics).* New Brunswick, N.J.: Rutgers University Press, 1999.

Smith, Norma. *Jeannette Rankin: America's Conscience.* Helena, Mont.: Montana Historical Society Press, 2002.

Tolchin, Susan. *Women in Congress, 1917–1976.* Washington, D.C.: Government Printing Office, 1976.

Wallace, Patricia Ward. *Politics of Conscience: A Biography of Margaret Chase Smith.* Westport, Conn.: Praeger, 1995.

Washington, Shirley. *Outstanding Women Members of Congress.* Washington, D.C.: U.S. Capitol Historical Society, 1995.

Woelfle, Gretchen. *Jeannette Rankin: Political Pioneer.* New York: Boyds Mills Press, 2007.

FILM

Chisholm '72: Unbought and Unbossed: An Interview with Schola Lynch. Realside Productions: 2004.

PAMPHLET

A. J. Muste Memorial Institute Pamphlet Essay Series.

WEBSITES

American Rhetoric. Top 100 Speeches: www.americanrhetoric.com

Encyclopedia of World Biography. www.notablebiographies.com

Jewish Women's Archive. www.jwa.org/encyclopedia

*Kids.Gov. www.kids.gov.comMargaret Chase Smith Library. www.mcslibrary.org

New Georgia Encyclopedia. www.georgiaencyclopedia.org

Oklahoma Historical Society's Encyclopedia of Oklahoma History and Culture. http://digital.library.okstate.edu/encyclopedia/index.html

San Francisco Chronicle. www.sfgate.com

United States Senate. www.senate.gov

*http://history.house.gov/Exhibition-and-Publications/WIC/Women-in-Congress. This book could not have been written without the website Women in Congress. This extensive, well-researched, well-written website holds more than just biographies of the women who have served in the U.S. House of Representatives and Senate. Based on the book *Women in Congress, 1917–2006*, the site also has historical essays that describe the cultural and political life of the country against which these women served. There are tables and appendices of historical data, links to information about current members, and resources for educators. The information that appears in "Complete List of Women in Congress" (pages 119–21) comes from this website.

Women of the West Museum. www.theautry.org

Women's History. www.about.com

Wikipedia. www.wikipedia.com

PHOTOGRAPHY CREDITS

SECTION OPENER PHOTOGRAPHS

Pages x–1: Library of Congress Prints and Photographs Division, Washington, D.C.; Harris & Ewing Collection. **Pages 12–13:** Franklin D. Roosevelt Presidential Library and Museum, Hyde Park, NY. **Pages 28–29:** Retrofile/Getty Images. **Pages 44–45:** Time & Life Pictures/Getty Images. **Pages 56–57:** Getty Images. **Pages 80–81:** Getty Images. **Pages 92–93:** Associated Press/Matt Rourke. **Pages 104–105:** Associated Press/Cliff Owen.

PORTRAITS OF WOMEN

Pages 5, 10, 18 (bottom), 19–21, 24, 26, 35, 40, 41, 50, 52, 55, 61, 63, 65, 67, 68, 70, 71, 72, 75, 107: Collection of the U.S. House of Representatives.

Pages 17, 33, 37, 77, 84, 89, 97, 101 (top left, bottom right): U.S. Senate Historical Office.

Pages 18 (top), 49: Library of Congress.

Page 54: Missouri State Archives.

Page 86 (top): Courtesy Susan B. Landrau.

Pages 86 (bottom), 87, 88, 89, 91, 100, 101 (top right, middle left, middle right), 102, 108–110: Courtesy of the member.

ACKNOWLEDGMENTS

The week before I graduated from high school, my mother died of a heart attack.

The salary she earned as a saleswoman was intended to cover my college tuition—thankfully much less in those days. Still, after her death, it seemed college might not be in the cards for me.

Then my family learned that we were entitled to her Social Security money. A few years earlier, this would not have been the case. While a man's Social Security money went to his family, a woman's was simply put back into the general fund.

It took a dedicated congresswoman, Martha Griffiths, to push for a bill that would reverse this injustice. In 1962, that bill became a law, and because it did, I was able to go to college and eventually become a writer. So, unlike some who question whether government can truly help people, I'm here to say I'm an example of someone who was helped by a legislator, a woman in this case, who was determined to make life better for the people of the United States.

A more recent way that government has helped me is in the writing of this book. Some of the information about U.S. congresswomen, especially those who served earliest (other than Jeannette Rankin, who is well documented), comes from the website Women in Congress 1917–1990. There is now an updated and expanded edition available: Women in Congress 1917–2006. This website was mandated by the House of Representatives in House Concurrent Resolution No. 66 by the 107th Congress, First Session. It was developed by the Office of History and Preservation under the Office of the Clerk of the U.S. House of Representatives. It is a treasure trove of women's history, political and otherwise, and it contains profiles of every woman who has served in Congress. I wish that I could have fit more of them within the pages of this book, because they each have a story to tell. I urge you take a look at this site. You will be fascinated.

This is not the first time I've written about women's political history. My very first book, *Susan B. Anthony* (New York: Franklin Watts, 1984), looked at the life of the great crusader for woman suffrage. I was able to use some of the research for that book here.

I would like to thank the terrific crew at Abrams Books for Young Readers, especially my perceptive editor, Howard Reeves, and the thoughtful staff: editorial assistant Melissa Faulner, managing editor Jim Armstrong, and designer Sara Edward Corbett. You all make beautiful books. Another big thank-you to marketing experts Jason Wells and Nicole Russo. And I'm especially grateful to copyeditor/fact-checker extraordinaire Renée Cafiero. Any mistakes in this book are my own, but Renée kept me honest.

I was thrilled and honored when I read Senator Olympia Snowe's foreword to this book. Senator Snowe represents the best of what women can do in Congress, and I hope that many girls and young women will eventually answer her call to become more involved in government.

INDEX

Note: Page numbers in *italics* refer to illustrations.

Abzug, Bella, 69–70, *70*, 71

Afghanistan, U.S. invasion of, 95

African Americans:
> civil rights for, 41, 42–43, 47–48, 49, 58–59

> Congressional Black Caucus, 67

> discrimination against, 73

> elected to office, 49, 60, 63, 65, 67, 85, 99

> and integration, 42–43, 52

> and presidential elections, 64, *93*, 96, 99

> segregation, *44–45*, 47

agriculture, 26, 34

Alaska, Murkowski from, 100

al-Qaeda, 94, 95

ambassadors, first woman, 27, 31, 41

Anthony, Susan B., 3, 114, 117

Arizona:
> Giffords from, 106

> voting rights in, 4

Arkansas:
> Caraway from, 30, 33–34

> Oldfield from, 34–35

> Wingo from, 35

armed forces, women's right to serve in, 21

Asian Americans, elected to office, 61, 109

Atomic Energy Commission, 41

Ayotte, Kelly, 110, *110*

Bachmann, Michele, 108, *108*

Baldwin, Tammy, 109, *109*

banking laws, 54

Berlin Wall, 82

bin Laden, Osama, 95

Blackmun, Harry A., *80–81*

Bloomer, Amelia, 3

Boehner, John, 106

Bolton, Chester, 50

Bolton, Frances Payne, 50–51, *50*

Bolton Act, 50–51

Booth, Ann, 40, 41

Boxer, Barbara, 86, *86*

Brennan, William J., Jr., *80–81*

Brooke, Edward, 85

Brown v. Board of Education, 47

Bryan, William Jennings, 25

Burger, Warren E., *80–81*

Burke, Yvonne Brathwaite, 67–68, *67*

Bush, George H. W., 39, 76, 83, 94

Bush, George W., 94, 95–96

Cabinet, presidential, 31, 117

Cadet Nurse Corps, U.S., 51

California:
> Boxer from, 86

> Burke from, 67, 68

> Douglas from, 41–42

> Feinstein from, 86

> Kahn from, 18–20

> Nolan from, 18–20

> Pelosi from, 102

> voting rights in, 4

Cantwell, Maria, 100, *100*

Capitol, U.S., viii, *viii, 1*, 52

Capone, Al, 15

Caraway, Hattie, 30, 33–34, *33*, 77

Caraway, Thaddeus, 33

Castro, Fidel, 88

Chisholm, Conrad, 63

Chisholm, Shirley, 63–64, *63*, 68

Church, Marguerite, 51–52, *52*

Church, Ralph, 51

civil rights, 32, 42, 47–48, 49, 52, 55, 58–59, 69, 70

Civil Rights Bill/Act, 55, 58–59

Civil War, U.S., end of, 47, 49

Clinton, Bill, 76, 83–84, 87, 94, 97–98, 101

Clinton, Chelsea, 97

Clinton, Hillary Rodham, *92*, 96, 97–99, *97*, 101

Cold War, 32, 50, 71, 82

Collins, Cardiss, 68, *68*

Collins, Susan, 89, 90–91, *91*

Colorado:
> Schroeder from, 72

> voting rights in, 4

> women legislators in, ix

Communism:
> anti-Communism, 38, 41, 82

> labeling people wrongly, 38–39, 43

> spread of, 32, 38, 43, 50

Congress:
> in each state, ix

> meanings of the word, ix

Congress, U.S.:
> African Americans in, 49, 60, 63, 65, 67, 85

Congress, U.S. (*cont.*)
    first Jewish woman in, 19
    first woman to chair a committee in, 19
    first woman to preside over, 11
    and JFK funeral, 48
    as Legislative Branch, viii, 112–13
    polarization in, 108
    roles of, 113
    women in, vi-vii, 47, 60, 62, 106, 109, 119–21
    and World War I, 6–8
    and World War II, 9
Congressional Black Caucus, 67
congressional committees, 116–18
Connecticut, Luce from, 39, 41
Constitution, U.S.:
    14th Amendment to, 114
    15th Amendment to, 114
    18th Amendment to, 14–15
    19th Amendment to, 3–4, 8, 17, 115, 117
    and elections, 85–86
    Equal Rights Amendment, 50, 55, 117–18
    Impeachment Clause, 118
    preamble to, 66
    speaker of the house, 102
    and Supreme Court, 114
    writing of, 112
consumer goods, 14
consumer protection laws, 53–54, 77
contracts, bidding on, 67–68
Creek Indians, 10
Cronkite, Walter, 71

Declaration of Conscience, 38
Defense Department, U.S., 73
Dellums, Ron, 73
Democratic National Committee, 65
Denmark, U.S. ambassador to, 27
Dole, Bob, 101
Dole, Elizabeth, 101, *101*
Douglas, Helen Gahagan, 36, 41–43, *41*
Douglas, Melvyn, 42
Duckworth, Tammy, 110, *110*
Dwyer, Florence, 49–50, *49*

education, 16, 18
    equal rights in, 62, 68
    Head Start, 64
    integration of, 47

education (*cont.*)
    nursing schools, 51
    scholarships, 51
Eisenhower, Dwight D., 39, 41
environmental activism, 87, 100
Equal Rights Amendment (ERA), 50, 55, 82, 117–18
Equal Rights Party, 3
Executive Branch, viii, 113

Fair Labor Standards Act, 22
Family and Medical Leave Act, 73
farm issues, 34
Federal Bureau of Investigation (F.B.I.), 20, 69
Federal Emergency Relief Administration (FERA)
    camp, *12–13*
Feinstein, Dianne, 86, *86*
Felton, Rebecca, 16–17, *17*, 22, 33
Felton, William, 16
feminists, 10
Fenwick, Millicent, 70–71, *71*
Ferraro, Geraldine, 75–76, *75*
Fischer, Deb, 109, *109*
flood control, 34
Florida:
    citrus trees in, 26
    election (2000) in, 94
    Owen from, 26–27, 31
Food and Drug Act, 53–54
Food Stamp Act, 54
foreign relations, 42, 52
Freedom Riders, 48
Friedan, Betty, 117

gay rights, 69
Georgia, Felton from, 16–17
Germany:
    Berlin Wall in, 82
    Nazi party in, 8
    and World War II, 8, 9
Giffords, Gabrielle, 106–7, *107*
Golden Gate Bridge, 20
Gorbachev, Mikhail, 82
Gore, Al, 94
Great Depression, 8, 15, 22, 24, 30, 32, 35, 42, 46
Great Society, 59, 62
Greensboro, North Carolina, 48
Griffiths, Hicks, 54
Griffiths, Martha Wright, 47, 54–55, *55*, 59, 128

gun control, 86
Hamilton, Alexander, 66
Hanna, Mark, 23, 24, 25
Hanna, Ruth (McCormick), 23–25, *24*
Hardwick, Thomas, 17
Hassan, Maggie, 110
Hawaii:
    Hirono from, 109
    Mink from, 61–62
Head Start, 64
health care, 8, 26, 50–51, 78, 87, 97, 98
Hébert, Edward, 73
Heitkamp, Heidi, 109, *109*
Hirono, Mazie, 109, *109*
Hispanic Americans, elected to office, 87
Hitler, Adolf, 8, 21
Holocaust, 21
Hoover, Herbert, 30
Hoover, J. Edgar, 20, 69
House of Representatives, state, ix
House of Representatives, U.S.:
    African Americans in, 49, 63, 65, 67, 68
    Appropriations Committee, 20
    Armed Services Committee, 37, 73
    Asian Americans in, 61
    Budget Committee, 75
    Judiciary Committee, 55, 65–66
    in Legislative Branch, viii, 112–13
    members in, ix
    Military Affairs Committee, 20
    Naval Affairs Committee, 37
    speaker of, 102–3, 106, 112–13
    Ways and Means Committee, 55
    women in, vi, 6, 8, 19–20, 22, 30, 35, 49, 61, 63, 69,
        87, *104–5*, 109–10, 119–21
Huck, Winnifred, 18, *18*
human rights abuses, 71
Humphrey, Hubert H., 60
Hunt, Jane, 114
Hussein, Saddam, 96
Hutchison, Kay Bailey, 100, *101*

Idaho, voting rights in, 4
"I Have a Dream" (King), 48
Illinois:
    African Americans elected from, 49
    Church from, 51
    Collins from, 68

Illinois (*cont.*)
    Hanna from, 24
    Huck from, 18
    McCormick from, 24
    Moseley Braun from, 85
    voting rights in, 24
immigration, 5
Iraq, war in, 18, 96, 110
Italy, U.S. ambassador to, 41

Japan, and World War II, 9
jobs:
    creation of, 31
    discrimination in, 59
Johnson, Lyndon B., 58, 59–60, 62, 66
Jordan, Barbara, 65–67, *65*, 68
Judicial Branch, viii, 113–14

Kahn, Florence, 18, 19–20, *19*, 21
Kahn, Julius, 19
Kansas:
    Kassebaum from, 77–79, 85
    voting rights in, 4
Kassebaum, Nancy Landon, 77–79, *77*, 85
Kelly, Mark, 107
Kennedy, Edward M. "Ted," 78
Kennedy, John F., 48, 52, 58
Kennedy, Robert F., 60
Kentucky, Langley from, 20
King, Rev. Martin Luther, Jr., 48, 60
Korean War, 18
Kuster, Ann McLane, 110, *110*

labor, organized, 42
Landon, Alf, 77
Landrieu, Mary, 100, *101*
Langley, Katherine, 20–21, *20*
legislation, passage of, 115–16
Legislative Branch (Congress), viii, 112–13
Library of Congress, U.S., 47
Lockwood, Belva, 3
Long, Huey "Kingfish," 34
Longworth, Alice Roosevelt, 20
Loughner, Jared, 107
Louisiana, Landrieu from, 100
Luce, Clare Boothe, 36, 39–41, *40*
Luce, Henry, 40

Maine:
 Collins from, 89, 90
 Smith from, 36–37
 Snowe from, 89, 108
Marshall, Thurgood, *80*
Maryland, Mikulski from, 21, 85, 88
Massachusetts:
 Rogers from, 20–21
 Warren from, 109
McCain, John, 96
McCarthy, Joseph, 38–39
McClintock, Mary Ann, 114
McCormick, Joseph Medill, 23–24
McCormick, Ruth Hanna, 23–25, *24*
McKernan, John, 89
McKinley, William, 23, 25
Mediterranean fruit fly, 26
Michigan:
 African Americans elected from, 49
 Griffiths from, 47, 55
 Stabenow from, 100
migrant workers, 42
Mikulski, Barbara, 21, 85, 88, *88*
Mink, John, 51
Mink, Patsy Takemoto, 61–62, *61*
Minnesota, Bachmann from, 108
Missouri, Sullivan from, 53–54
Mondale, Walter, 75–76
Montana:
 Rankin from, 5–9
 voting rights in, 4, 6
Montgomery, Alabama, civil rights in, 47
Moseley Braun, Carol, 85, *85*
Mott, Lucretia, 3
movies, talking pictures, 14
Murkowski, Lisa, 100, *101*
Murray, Patty, 87, *87*, 100

National Council for Prevention of
 War, 8
Native Americans:
 teachers of, 10
 welfare of, 11
Nebraska, Fischer from, 109
Negroes, use of term, 47
Neuberger, Maurine, 77, *77*
Nevada, voting rights in, 4
New Deal, 31, 34

New Hampshire:
 Ayotte from, 110
 Kuster from, 110
 Shaheen from, 110
 Shea-Porter from, 110
New Jersey:
 Dwyer from, 49–50
 Fenwick from, 70
 Norton from, 21–22
Newtown, Connecticut, school shooting in, 86
New York:
 Abzug from, 69
 African Americans elected from, 49
 Chisholm from, 63
 Clinton elected from, 98
 Ferraro from, 75
 September 11 attacks in, 94–95, *95*, 98
Nixon, Richard M., 39
 election of, 60
 first president to resign, 43, 60, 66, 118
 impeachment trial of, 65, 69
 as "Tricky Dick," 43
 and Watergate, 43, 60, 65, 69
Nolan, Mae, 18–19, *18*
North Carolina, Dole from, 101
North Dakota, Heitkamp from, 109
Norton, Mary, 21–22, *21*, 46
nuclear arms race, 32

Obama, Barack, *93*, 96, 99
O'Connor, Sandra Day, 80, *81*
Ohio, Bolton from, 50
Oklahoma:
 Robertson from, 10–11
 territory of, 10
 voting rights in, 4
Oldfield, Pearl, 20, 34–35, *35*
Oldfield, William, 34
Oregon:
 Neuberger from, 77
 voting rights in, 4
Owen, Ruth Bryan, 25–27, *26*, 31

pacifists, 7, 18
Parks, Rosa, 47
Paul, Alice, 118
peace, 8–9, 41
Peace Corps, 52

Pearl Harbor, Japanese attack on, 9

Pearson, James, 78

Pelosi, Nancy, 102–3, *102*

Pennsylvania:

    FERA camp in, *12–13*

    September 11 attack in, 95

Perkins, Frances, 31

Perot, H. Ross, 83

Persian Gulf War, 83

political parties, 115

politics:

    frustrations in, 19

    job of, 42

    and politicians, 115

poverty, 59, 67

Powell, Adam Clayton, Jr., 49

Powell, Lewis F., Jr., *80–81*

presidency:

    candidacy for, 39, 64, *92–93*, 98–99, 101, 108

    different kinds of men in, 82

    election challenged (2000), 94

    Executive Branch, viii, 113

    and impeachment, 65, 66, 69, 83–84, 118

    veto power, 116

Presidential Medal of Freedom, 39, 41

press, freedom of, 32

Prohibition, 14–15, 27

propaganda, 32

property ownership, 2

racial issues, 16–17

    apartheid, 51, 79

    bus boycott, 47

    Civil Rights Bill/Act, 55, 58–59

    Freedom Riders, 48

    "I Have a Dream," 48

    integration, 42–43, 52

    lunch counter sit-ins, 47–48

    segregation, 42–43, *44–45*, 47, 61

    Voting Rights Act, 59

radio, invention of, 14

Rankin, Jeannette, *4*, 5–9, *5*, 10, 16, 18, 21, 30

Reagan, Ronald, 41, 73, 76, 82–83, 101

"Red Menace," 32

Rehnquist, William H., *81*

religion, freedom of, 32

reproductive rights, 69

Republican Party, moderates in, 91

Robertson, Alice Mary, 10–11, *10*, 16, 22

Rogers, Edith Nourse, 20–21, *21*, 22

Rogers, John, 21

Roosevelt, Eleanor, 31, 42

Roosevelt, Franklin Delano, 9, 27, 31, 34, 41, 42, 77

Roosevelt, Theodore "Teddy," 10, 20

"Rosie the Riveter," 32

Ros-Lehtinen, Ileana, 87–88, *88*

Rough Riders, 10

San Francisco–Oakland Bay Bridge, 20

Schroeder, Patricia, 72–74, *72*, 75

science and technology, 41

Senates, state, ix

Senate, U.S.:

    Appropriations Committee, 86

    first woman in, 16

    first woman to preside over, 34

    Foreign Relations Committee, 79

    impeachment vote in, 84, 118

    in Legislative Branch, viii, 113

    members in, ix

    Select Committee on Intelligence, 86

    women in, vi, 16, 17, 30, 33, 37–38, 85, 86, 100, 119–21

Seneca Falls, New York, 3, 114

September 11 attacks, 94–95, *95*, 98

Shaheen, Jeanne, 110, *110*

Shea-Porter, Carol, 110, *110*

Smith, Clyde, 37

Smith, Margaret Chase, vi, 36–39, *37*, 48, 77, 90

Snowe, Olympia, vi-vii, *vi*, 89–90, *89*, 91, 108

Snowe, Peter, 89

Social Security, 31, 55

South Africa, apartheid in, 51, 79

South Dakota, voting rights in, 4

Soviet Union (Russia), 32, 38, 82

Spanish-American War, 10

special elections, 17, 18, 19, 21, 33

speech, freedom of, 32

spies, 32

Stabenow, Deborah, 100, *101*

Stanton, Elizabeth Cady, 3, 114, 117

Stevens, John Paul, *80–81*

stock market crash, 15, 30

Stone, Lucy, 117

suffrage movement, *1*, 2–4, 6

Sullivan, Leonor K., 53–54, *54*

Supreme Court, U.S., viii, 47, *80–81*, 113–14
  O'Connor appointed to, 82–84
  and presidential election (2000), 94
swing voters, 91

Taft, William Howard, 25
television, women shown on, 46
terrorism, 94–95
Texas:
  Hutchison from, 100
  Jordan from, 65, 67
Touchdown Club, 72, 74

unemployment, *12–13*, 30
United Nations (UN), and equal rights, 51
U.S. Commission on Immigration Reform, 67
Utah, voting rights in, 4

veterans, elected to office, 110
veterans' benefits, 11, 21, 87
Vietnam War, 9, 18, 59–60, 62, 64, 69
voting rights:
  for African Americans, 49, 59
  roadblocks to, 59
  for women, *1*, 2–4, 6, 8, 10, 16, 17, 24, *56–57*, 114–15, 117
Voting Rights Act, 59

wage:
  equal pay, 37, 50, 54
  fair, 18–19, 22
  minimum, 22
War on Poverty, 59
Warren, Elizabeth, 109, *109*
Washington (state):
  Cantwell from, 100
  Murray from, 87, 100
  voting rights in, 4, 6
Washington, D.C.:
  racial issues in, 42–43
  September 11 attack on, 95
Washington, George, 66
Watergate, 43, 60, 65, 69
White, Byron R., *80–81*
Whitewater, 97–98
Wilson, Pete, 86
Wilson, Woodrow, 7, 17
Wingo, Effiegene, 35, *35*

Wisconsin, Baldwin from, 109
women:
  abuse of, 15
  in the armed services, 73
  civil rights for, 2–4, 10–11, 41, 55, 60, 62, 70, 72, 110–11
  discrimination against, 72–73
  dual roles of, 62
  filling fathers' seats in Congress, 16, 18
  filling husbands' seats in Congress, 16, 18, 21, 33, 35, 37, 46, 50, 52–53, 68, 77
  and glass ceiling, 103
  jobs for, 2, 31–32, 63–64, 111
  maternity leave for, 67
  nurses, 37, 51
  "old maids," 2
  as presidential candidates, 3, 39
  reproductive rights for, 69, 78
  role models for, 36, 46
  as silent majority, vi
  sports programs for, 62, 68
  in Supreme Court, *80–81*, 82–84
  on television, 46
  traditional roles of, 2, 46, 48, 54, 72, 111, 114
  unemployed, *12–13*
  vice presidential candidacy of, 75–76
  voting rights for, *1*, 2–4, 6, 8, 10, 16, 17, 24, *56–57*, 114–15, 117
  "Year of the Woman," 84, 87, 88, 110
Women, The (Luce), 40
women's issues, vii, 8, 10, 16, 18, 26, 55, 67, 69, 70, 73, 75
women's movement, 3, 114, 117
Woodhull, Victoria, 3
working conditions, 22
Works Progress Administration (W.P.A.), 31
World War I, 6–8, 11, 14
World War II, 8–9, 22, 42
  aircraft assembly in, *28–29*, 32
  end of, 30, 32, 38, 43, 46
  female reporters in, 40
  jobs in, *28–29*, 31–32, *32*
  nurses in, 51
Wright, Martha, 114
Wyoming, voting rights in, 4

"Year of the Woman," 84, 87, 88, 110